W0038338

Growing Up in Bavaria

Marita Barker

© 2021 Marita Barker

All rights reserved. This book or any portion thereof may not be reproduced or used in any manner whatsoever without the express written permission of the publisher except for the use of brief quotations in a book review.

ISBN: 978-1-09836-509-7

GROWING UP IN BAVARIA

For a long time, I had been contemplating writing down some of my memories and family history but had always put it off. My friend Bara invited me to attend our community Writers Club open house, where I heard someone say, *"There are all these stories in your head and, unless you write them down, they will die with you."* That comment finally prompted me to write this book and share some stories of what it was like growing up in Bavaria.

I hope you enjoy reading about my childhood, parents, and siblings and – in the process – understand some of the things that shaped me. I am also giving you a glimpse into my family's background.

This little bit of history is dedicated to my children Scott, Doree, and Melodi; my grandchildren Robin, Courtney, Candis, Raquel, Britny, Jay, Schuyler, Tanya, Heyley, Dylan, Nicolas, Steven, and Alia and their families; and my nieces Carola and Sandy and their families.

It felt so good being able to collaborate with my sister Freda on some of the stories and tidbits. The comment "do you remember?" was often the beginning of reliving some great and sometimes sad memories. Thank you, Sissy!

A special thank you to my husband, Mal, for encouraging and supporting me to do this! Your help scanning and fixing old photos plus providing me with other pictures taken over the years helped to make this book that much more special.

Contents

Chapter 1

Bavaria

Bavaria is where I grew up. It is the largest state in Germany, often referred to as the most beautiful. Bavaria is situated in the southeast and covers almost one-fifth of the country's total land area, encompassing 70,548 square kilometers (27,200 square miles). Bavaria shares borders with Austria, the Czech Republic, Switzerland, and Poland. And it is easy to visit nearby Italy, France, and Liechtenstein.

Bavaria is home to the Alps, one of the largest mountain ranges in the world. The tallest peak is Zugspitze, whose summit reaches 9,718 feet, the highest point of elevation in Germany. Some of my favorite mountains that I visited on several occasions are Hochplatte, Hochgern, Hochfeln, and Kampenwand.

Farmers send their cows up to the Alps from spring to fall. The *Almhuetter*, the person or persons taking care of the cows, can really enjoy the beauty and the tranquility. Of course, there is a festive Bavarian parade when they come home in the fall.

The Alps are home to three flowers. Edelweiss is a white star-shaped flower; the blue bell-shaped blossom is Enzian; and Alpen-Röschen is a pink spray of blooms. Edelweiss grows on the highest peaks, and you marvel at the lack of soil it grows in. When my parents were growing up, it was still a tradition that the bridegroom would pick Edelweiss for his bride's bouquet the day before their wedding. The mountains can be treacherous, especially at twilight; and many sad songs have been composed about accidents that took a groom's life.

Bavaria has four true seasons, and the transitions between them are fabulous. The blue skies and the white snow caps on the Alps are breathtaking. Some of the snow caps on the higher mountains are there year-round. In the spring, the meadows are a lush green with abundant wildflowers and wild berries. In the summer you see the wheat swaying with the wind; and in the fall the trees showcase the most beautiful shades of yellow, orange, red, and brown. As you drive through Bavaria you will find numerous *Marterl* (a memorial in honor of someone that lost their life on that particular spot). Some are plain while others are very beautiful. Sometimes they have a name, picture; or date; other times they are anonymous.

Visitors always seem to be amazed how clean the streets are. In Bavaria it is a given that you clean and, if necessary, scrub the sidewalk in front of your house.

Bavaria has a rich royal history. As I young girl, I loved watching movies capturing some of those times, especially the movies about Sissy (Elizabeth), a Bavarian princess and later Empress of Austria and Queen of Hungary by marriage to Emperor Franz Joseph I. It was a true love story. Sissy was also cousin to King Ludwig II, who occupied and built several castles in Bavaria including Herrenchiemsee and Neuschwanstein in the Alps. Visitors to those castles still provide an incredible amount of income to the State of Bavaria.

Bavaria is known as the vacation state of Germany. Its history, traditions, natural beauty, flowers, sports possibilities, and cleanliness plus the friendliness of its people continue to lure visitors to explore Bavaria and its capital, Munich.

Chapter 2

Chiemgau and the Chiemsee

Chiemgau is the area around Chiemsee, which is where our family is from. Chiemsee is referred to as *"Das Bayrische Meer"* (the Bavarian Ocean) as it is the largest lake in Bavaria. I believe 1922 was the last time the entire lake froze to a point that a horse-drawn wagon could cross from the mainland to the islands. It is written that, when it started to warm up and the ice started cracking, frightening sounds were heard. Locals said the lake was barking.

Storms in this area come up quickly. Many times people in small rowboats find themselves in dangerous conditions, and the lake claims its victims each year. I remember that, when lightning storms came, we closed the shutters, turned off the lights, and used a special candle for illumination as we prayed until the worst of the storm had passed. It was common for the lightning actually to hit the ground and roll like a fiery ball in a straight line, setting on fire whatever was in its way.

Chiemsee

The lake has three islands. The smallest is called Kraut Insel because only vegetation grows there.

The next largest is Fraueninsel. A large part of this island is home to a convent and a beautiful baroque-style church surrounded by a traditional cemetery. German graves are tended to meticulously. Most of the time they have been planted with greenery and flowers. Many have candle holders and a holy water dispenser. It is not uncommon for others to tend someone's grave when the deceased no longer has living relatives in the area – just another way that people take care of each other and show their pride in appearance.

Picture of Fraueninsel

This island is the only place the fabulously delicious Chiemseer Kloster liqueur is made. The liqueur is made by nuns who reside there and run the restaurants. The liqueur can only be purchased at the island and in a few villages that access the island by boat. I wish I could get some of the liqueur here; it comes in a few different flavors, and *halb-bitter* is my personal favorite.

The largest island is Herren Chiemsee. Duke Tassilo III of Bavaria established a monastery as well as a convent there in 782. The Huns devastated most of the island in the first half of the 10th century. In 969 Emperor Otto the Great donated the Abbey to the Bishop of Salzburg. After changing hands several times, the island was auctioned off in 1803 to Carl von Luenenschloss for 39,500 florins. Being a smart businessman, Luenenschloss turned a quick profit by selling it for 52,000 florins to Aloys von Fleckinger, at which time the Abbey was turned into a brewery. In September 1873, King Ludwig II of Bavaria (also known as the fairytale king) finally purchased the island as a site to erect his palace. King Ludwig II was a big admirer of King Louis XIV of France and built his castle to resemble Versailles.

I have visited this castle on many occasions. It is truly magnificent. Most impressive is the ball room, also known as the hall of mirrors. There are 17 arched windows located between red pilasters. They are opposite a wall hung with huge mirrors. The chandeliers with an incredible number of candles are magnificent. I always marveled at the beauty and architecture of the castle.

Castle Herrenchiemsee

King Ludwig II was a recluse and did not like people around. Consequently he modified his dining room so that the table could be set on the lower floor in the kitchen and then elevated with pulleys to the dining room. Ludwig was also a big supporter of Richard Wagner, and we would not have Wagner's music if not for the king. Ludwig was mesmerized by Wagner's compositions and took over all of Wagner's financial burdens, built a villa for him, and provided him with the freedom and peace of mind to compose his music. The castle holds the world's largest music box that contains only Wagner's music. My children Scott and Doree, and my niece Carola, all had the privilege of visiting the islands and touring the castle in 1980 with my sister Freda and me.

There are several interesting books written about King Ludwig II and his continuing impact on Bavaria. The king's construction of expensive castles and other installations over a period of 20 years impaired the state budget tremendously. Consequently, there was a coup in which Ludwig II was declared insane and sent into exile to the Berg Castle on Starnberg Lake, where he subsequently drowned in 1886 along with his physician. The mystery of how they died still remains.

Today we could define the reign of Ludwig II as the "golden century" for Bavarian culture, especially music. The king constructed not only castles and palaces, but also theatres and galleries. He founded the Bavarian Red Cross, the Munich Polytechnic University, the Academy of Fine Arts, and the fund for development of music culture, which later laid the foundations for the famous Wagner festivals in Bayreuth in the specially constructed Wagner opera theatre.

Chapter 3

Chieming

After our parents were married in 1939, they moved to Pfaffing, on the outskirts of Chieming and later built their home in Chieming.

Chieming is located on the shores of Chiemsee. The view is spectacular! Visitors marvel at the beauty of the Alps. The peaks of Hochfelln and Hochgern were the view from our house and what I saw from my balcony bedroom. From the lake, our view of the Kampenwand was spectacular. The sunsets with the reflections in the water were unforgettable. Sometimes I try to remember, why did I leave there? Oh yes, I was in love!

Pictures of Chiemsee

Chieming was one of the first settlements in the lower Alps and can be traced back to Roman times. The name came from Duke Ciemo, who built Schloss Chiembing, later renamed Chieming.

When I was about six years old, only 300 people lived in Chieming. Our beautiful church was in the center of the town. We had two grocery stores, one next to the church and one across the street. City Hall and the school were located across from the church as well. The school also housed the apartment of the school principal and his family. We also had a bakery, butcher shop, shoemaker, blacksmith, two nurseries, grain store, bank, gas station with auto repair shop, and paint shop. We also had a doctor, dentist, and post office plus, as time went on, we even got a movie theater that was open in the summertime.

Our two restaurants had excellent food. Oberwirt was located next to the post office and bus stop at the entrance to town, and Unterwirt was down the hill by the lake. Unterwirt also housed the hall we used for traditional dancing, theatre, and gymnastics. Dad enjoyed being in numerous theatre performances there. Freda, the lead dancer in the traditional dancing group, would go there for practices and performances. I will never forget being part of gymnastics there; the parallel bars were my favorite.

But our town would not have been complete without a huge soccer field. I never got too interested in soccer but was often there with my friend Rosl to hold the cold drinks for the players. Theo was our star, and he later married Rosl.

As time went on, Herzinger Barbl opened a little place where she sold Bavarian gift items, postcards, toys, and craft items. She was very talented and taught crafts. As the town grew, additional stores and little cafés popped up. By 2010 Chieming had already grown to 2,000 people. A stroll through the city would give you a flavor of the pride everyone took in their houses. Many buildings had huge religious or traditional paintings on the street-facing wall and of course sported beautiful flowers on their balconies.

One thing unique to Chieming was that we had only one police officer. His mode of transportation was a bicycle. Our postman also delivered mail by bicycle. He had a big brown leather pouch with a lid affixed to the front of it. Our bikes all had baskets in front and in back as that was the transportation used for most of our shopping.

Families in my hometown were all involved in local traditions, music, dancing, boating, fishing, swimming, sports, art and, of course, the beautiful outdoors. Children could always count on encouragement and support from their parents. It was heartwarming to see young and old involved in activities together.

Chieming am Chiemsee

Chapter 4

My Parents' Courtship

My mom worked from 1930 to 1932 as a maid for a farmer named Sailer in the village of Kammer. She earned 5 Reichsmark per week, equivalent to about 2 US Dollars at that time. She worked the fields and the stable. One time when the farmer's wife was having a baby, my mom was asked to handle the kitchen and cook for everyone. They all raved about the food, and after that she was often asked to cook the *Mittagessen* (supper), the biggest meal of the day.

In 1932 mom was asked by a farmer named Hauser, in nearby Frabertsham, to come to work for them as a housemaid. No stable work was required, and she got a pay raise to 7 Reichsmark per week. Mom stayed there until she got married. In later years, she often visited the Hauser family in Frabertsham; and I was able to go with her. She was always treated like family, never like a former maid.

It was in 1931 at the age of 18 that she joined the Gebirgs und Volkstrachten Erhaltungs Verein, a formal club that performed traditional Bavarian dances. My mom was about 5'2" tall, and she had long blonde braids that she wrapped around her head Bavarian-style. She loved music and dancing and had an incredible sense of humor and an infectious laugh.

It is at that club she met my dad. He also worked nearby at a farm and spent a lot of his days with the horses, which he loved. He, too, loved music and dancing and had just joined the club. At age 21 and 5'10" tall, this handsome, strong, and dark-haired man caught my mom's attention right away. Her spunky personality and her love for dancing caught my dad's attention immediately.

I remember mom lighting up when she reminisced about that time in their lives, and the same was true for dad. I would have loved to hear more about those days. Every once in a while, they would exchange a mischievous smile and tell me a little tidbit of a story such as dad climbing up the ladder to mom's bedroom window for a kiss. He could not climb in, just get a kiss, that was the rule in that tradition during the courtship. This is called "*Fensterln*," and there is also a traditional dance called *Fensterln*.

The traditional dances must be performed in a very precise manner; and there are many different dances such as crown dance, braid dance, courtship dance, *Fensterln*, woodchopper's dance, and of course *Schuhplatteln*. The lead couple gives various signals to keep everyone on track. The lead couple is key to the quality of the performance.

Somehow mom and dad got paired. And it was not long before they were promoted to the lead. I can only imagine the great times and fun they had. Over the years they traveled to various cities in Bavaria to perform, and their club was even written up in a book (my sister Freda has the book) for the fabulous performances. By the way, Freda inherited their love for music and talent for dancing.

Mom wearing
her Trachte

Dad
in Lederhosen

The women wore what is called *Trachte*, a garment that includes a dress, apron, blouse, and a shawl. The colors are different for each area or county. In our area the colors were black and a light sky blue. There were several groups in each Club: children, women, and older women. The middle group in our area wore fresh flowers like my mom has on in the picture above. The older group wore special hats. In our area they were covered with black velvet, embroidered with gold threads, and embellished with small pearls and beads. The boys and men all wore lederhosen; depending on the time of year, they would be short or below the knee.

Mom and dad dated for eight years. Dad bought mom a ring with her initials, TK, and in turn mom bought one for dad with his initials, AR. They wore these rings as a token of belonging to one another. Mom kept hoping that her parents would consent to the marriage; however, they greatly resisted because dad was only a *Knecht* (farm hand). Mom's parents had picked Andreas, a man a bit older than my mom, as her future husband. Andreas worked for the post office and eventually would get a pension. But mom's heart belonged to dad, and she held out. Finally, on June 3, 1939, they were married; and her parents reluctantly agreed and attended the wedding.

A very small reception was held at Goriwirt in Egerer (Mom's hometown). Because it was wartime, Mom chose a black dress and white veil instead of the traditional white wedding dress out of respect for the fallen soldiers.

My parents' wedding picture

Shortly after the wedding, mom and dad moved to Pfaffing, a very small village on the outskirts of Chieming and about two miles from mom's family.

Chapter 5

Building Our House

We lived in a house in Pfaffing with five other families. The house belonged to a Baroness, Frau Josten, who was property rich and money poor. The house had long ago been converted from what I believe was a farmhouse into an L-shaped apartment building. We lived upstairs in the front and could reach out of the bedroom window to the climbing pear tree.

In the front downstairs lived the Kotzinger family with their two children, Rita and George. Rita was a little older than Freda, and George was about Freda's age. Sadly, George was killed. He was at the St. George fair to celebrate his birthday and dropped his money. As he bent over to pick it up, he got hit in the temple by a gondola. It was devastating and Kotzi mama, as we lovingly called her, never totally recovered from that tragedy.

Frau Hoepke, with her daughter Christine and sons Fritz and Eberhart, occupied apartment number three. Herr Mayer, a retired post office employee, and his wife had apartment number four. The largest apartment belonged to Frau Josten.

I think my dad always tried to prove to mom's parents that he was a good provider and that mom was better off being married to the man she loved instead of the man they had picked for her. Dad was a very ingenious person. By 1949, things were not yet easy as everyone was still trying to recover from the war. Mom and dad were hardworking individuals, and they wanted to build a house. However, after paying rent and taking care of all the necessities, there was no money left over to build or buy. Freda was eight years old and I was almost four. Mom was doing some domestic labor for the Baroness to help bring in a little money. Frau Josten was always very satisfied with mom's work. So my parents approached the Baroness with a proposition. Mom would provide domestic labor such as cooking, cleaning, laundry, and ironing; and dad would provide her with firewood for a period of five years in exchange for a half-acre lot catty corner across the street. The negotiation was successful!

Dad went to the forestry department, which was in charge of cutting forest trees, and offered to remove tree stumps at no charge in exchange for the stump wood. They accepted. Dad perfected a way of removing the stumps, and that's how he was able to get the firewood at no cost.

Mom did the cooking, cleaning, laundry, and ironing for the Baroness; and they had a great relationship. They cared for and respected each other. At the end of the five years, Frau Josten gave Mom a Bernstein (amber) charm in a silver facing along with the chain as a token of her gratitude and friendship.

In case you are curious what amber is, I will tell you. Amber is approximately 40 - 60 million years old and was held dear by many ancient cultures, treasured both for its protective and decorative qualities. Amber is actually not a stone, but rather amorphous, fossilized tree sap. It comes in a variety of yellow, orange, and sunny brown tones and ranges from transparent to semi-translucent. It was one of the first substances used for personal adornment. In fact, decorated pieces of amber have been found in remains from the Stone Age.

Mom and Dad started working on building the house during the five years. After their normal workdays and on weekends, they dug the basement by hand. They did not have fancy equipment available nor the money to buy or rent it. During that time, mom got pregnant with my brother but did not allow this to slow her down. It was always work as usual. There was always something for Freda and me to do, we did not sit idle. Manfred was the only one still too young to help, so sometimes I had the chore of keeping him occupied.

Once the basement was dug, we started on the blocks. The process required mixing sand and cement in about a six-foot-long row and then making a well on top in the middle. Either Freda or I used a watering can pour the water into the well, and our parents would mix it all together. It was very interesting the way it was done, shoveling from the right to the center first, and then the next shovel from the left to the center. Dad and mom started from the sides until they met in the middle. This process was repeated until the consistency was right.

If Dad was busy with other things, Freda and mom would do the mixing and I the watering. The mixture would then be put in a mold that looked similar to a cinder block. The mold was about 18" x 10" and had a divider inside to create two air chambers, which served as the insulation when it was used to build a house. Dad had a stomping tool to compress the mixture in the mold. Once unmolded, the blocks had to be cured by watering them and then letting them dry out several times.

Dad sold the first set of 500 blocks, which brought him enough money to buy the materials we needed to make enough blocks for the house. But constructing our house was a slow process. My parents each worked their regular jobs, weather conditions varied, and funds were not always available. After about four and a half years, though, we had what is called a *rohbau*: basically, the walls were built but the roof, windows, and doors were still missing. Our neighbor, Klausner, who was a pig and cow farmer at the time, was redoing his pig stable. Mom asked him what his plans were for the old windows, and he replied that he had no need for them. So mom asked him to let us have them, and he did.

After the war, dad had secured a job with Ellmaier, the local furniture maker in our village. He worked for him for two years and then needed to seek other employment. After all, how much furniture can you sell in a small village? Dad's next job was working for Thiele in Traunstein. Thiele was a very successful home builder. The knowledge dad acquired proved to be incredibly valuable in building our house from beginning to end. Dad built the window frames and was able to use the glass from the stable for all the windows in the house. He also made all the doors. Mom was right there with him, following his instructions. Those two were an incredible team, always pulling that wagon together.

When the house was all done except the roof, Dad was helping Klausner out in the field. I don't know how the accident happened, but the tractor went over Dad's foot, putting him out of commission for a while. Well, there are many benefits to living in a small village where neighbors help neighbors. For us, this was a special blessing at that time as our neighbors got together and put the roof on our house. And in 1953, five years after negotiating with Frau Josten, we moved into our home. There was no more rent to be paid, and we were mortgage-free. My mom's parents finally realized that my mom had picked the right husband!

Now mom's work started. She painted, sewed curtains and pillows, and did all the things needed to make the house a beautiful home. Dad built a balcony with fancy railings and flower boxes. And mom filled the boxes with beautiful flowers. As time went on, they added a chicken coop and pig stable, plus eventually a two-car garage and a carving room for Dad.

The view from the house was unobstructed and breathtaking. You could see Hochgern and Hochfelln, two mountains in the Alps that you may have seen in the opening scene of the Sound of Music. Below is a picture of what it all looked like after everything was completed: the house, garden, balcony, shutters, flower boxes, and flowers. The upstairs room where the umbrella is open was my room except during summer rental. The furniture in that room was painted light blue and had flowers that decorated it. I loved it!

Chapter 6

Food and Flowers

People in our village tried to be as self-sufficient as possible as far as food was concerned while at the same time showing pride in their homes and gardens. Mom had a green thumb, another thing my sister Freda inherited. Our garden had everything from butterleaf lettuce, tomatoes, radishes, carrots, cauliflower, and cucumbers to green onions, rhubarb, herbs, and other seasonal vegetables including kohlrabi. I still love munching on a raw kohlrabi. When it was time to make a salad, mom would just tell us what to get from the garden. We were spoiled, we had the freshest of fresh.

We had currant and gooseberry bushes that formed a fence at the back part of the garden. I loved eating the berries and rhubarb. All I needed was a little bit of sugar. Yum, what a sweet treat! Strawberries were always abundant; we grew them for Aunt Marie. She needed them to make her wonderful pastries for the café she and her husband, Hans, owned. Because I love strawberries, they always looked so good and it was hard not to pick some and just put them in my mouth. But they were not for us to eat.

The street side of the garden showcased beautiful flowers. Pink and dark pink peonies were planted along the fence, and they were mom's pride and joy. Hollyhocks in various colors outlined the parameter of the raised patio. And depending on the time of year, we had sunflowers, dahlias, marigolds, geraniums, pansies, daffodils, snowbells, hyacinths and, of course, violets and forgetmenots. The colors were so beautifully paired, and the fragrance was incredible.

It was a family affair to create a dwarf garden. Mom sent us kids to collect shells at the lake. Dad arranged them in a flower pattern in cement stones to support the little hill. Mom planted little flowers and used a mirror to give the illusion of a lake, then she placed a dwarf with a fishing rod at the edge. Other dwarfs and of course Snow White were strategically placed as well. It was magical!

Dad made a little house with doors and windows and Seeoner Opa, his father, made a windmill as his contribution. Mom would sit down with us every spring to repaint the dwarfs to keep them looking new. I reminisce about that time each spring when I repaint my garden ceramics.

People always marveled at the beauty of our garden. Since many people from northern Germany spent their summer vacations in Bavaria, the city encouraged the beautiful maintenance of front yards by giving awards. The top award was not having to pay property taxes for that year. Mom received that award for several years.

For protein sources we raised chickens. If someone very special came to visit, mom would catch a chicken and that would be our dinner. I understood, but did not like being there. I guess some of those farm chores just were not my calling even then.

When little chicks hatched during a cold spell, mom would put the chicks in a cardboard box and bring them in the kitchen. We would then hard-boil eggs and chop them ever so tiny to feed the chicks. I remember my little brother, Manfred, squealing with delight. They were so sweet, fluffy, yellow, and adorable.

Each year we got a piglet from Klausner and raised it. That was one of our sources of meat and sausage. Once a year the local butcher, Metzger Sepp, came to the house to slaughter the pig. I understood why this had to be done, but I just could not be at home when it happened. Egerer Opa would come to make the sausages. I must say, he used just the right kind of seasoning and made the best darn sausages. There was always help needed in that process, such as preparing the natural casings or holding the casings open for Opa to pour in the sausage mixture. I hated it. Freda, being the elder, ended up having to do those chores.

Dad went hunting for rabbits. Later he raised rabbits in the back of the house, some for food and others that he would sell.

I loved going with dad to the forest for mushrooms. He taught me to search on the moss side of the trees to find the best and biggest mushrooms, and he was very specific about which mushrooms to pick and which not to touch or pick, as they were poisonous. Mom did not like mushrooms herself but would make an awesome mushroom sauce and bread dumplings when we got home. Absolutely delicious!

Chapter 7

The School System

Our schoolhouse was in the center of the village and contained classrooms from 1st grade to 8th. Because we were a small town, two grades were always combined into one. The schedule was Monday through Friday from 8 am to 5 pm, and Saturday from 8 am to 1 pm. We got a one-week break at Christmas, another one week at Easter, and six weeks off in the summer. After 8th grade, we graduated from *Volksschule*, which is equivalent to high school in America.

Below is a picture of me on my first day at school in 1951. It was customary to get a fancy container full of candy on your first day of school. Mine was borrowed for this picture as that was not in the budget. However, I don't think it bothered me a bit. I look pretty happy.

In 5th and 6th grades, I had a very interesting teacher, Herr Angerer. He always taught math in the first hour. I must have been good in math, because at least once a week he sent me to his house during that time to help his wife with chores. She would always give me money as a thank you, which he promptly took from me when I got back to school. So, one day I asked her if she could please give me an apple instead. They had a wonderful apple tree, and she was glad to do that. That's the day I learned how to break an apple in half. I gave Herr Angerer only one half and kept the other. The look on his face was priceless!

My sister Freda had him as her teacher four years earlier. He had a ruler embellished with thumbtacks. He liked slapping your hand with it and drawing a little blood if you were not paying attention. Ouch! Freda encountered that a couple of times, but I was lucky enough not ever to be on the receiving end of that ruler. One time Freda got in trouble because she only had one notebook, and Herr Angerer demanded that each student have a separate notebook for each subject instead of just dividers. Dad paid him a visit and informed him in no uncertain terms that we could not afford to buy all those notebooks and, if he wanted Freda to have them, he was welcome to buy them for her.

All teachers had their own way to make sure they had your attention. Our Priest, Pfarrer Brandstaetter, was very strict. If you were not paying attention or were disruptive, he would find a little bunch of hair by your ear, then twist and pull until it brought tears to your eyes. He could be mean! I usually managed to stay out of trouble.

Don't get the wrong idea, we had some great teachers. My favorite was Herr Hager. He later became our mayor and married a waitress called Fuescherl (which means foxy). She was a redhead, and her name fit her to a tee. Herr Hager was my 7th grade teacher and was instrumental in convincing my parents to let me skip a grade and go to *Mittelschule* Sparz for my degree. He was strict but fair, and he always had the best for the community and its people in mind.

I remember visiting Herr Hager in the hospital on one of our visits to Germany. He was in his last weeks on this earth. It was heartbreaking to see him lying there all frail, a man I remember as strong, an incredible soccer player who loved life. His eyes lit up as he held my hand, grateful for the visit! It meant the world to me when he said that I was always one of his favorites! After we left the hospital, my husband, Mal, held me as I wept.

The school was there for the community in times of need. I remember one year when we had an invasion of potato bugs. The school sent all of us kids with jars to collect potato bugs to save the crops for the farmers. It was considered a school outing. In retrospect, what a wonderful way to help and support each other.

Once you graduated from high school and had picked your profession, you were required to attend *Berufsschule* (trade school) one day per week for three years. It was schooling specific to your job. A florist would become a flower specialist; a beautician would learn everything about hair; and if you were a farmer's daughter, for instance, and did not seek a job, you would still go to trade school and learn to cook, can, sew, etc. My sister Freda attended trade school to become a chef in a restaurant in northern Germany. High school and trade school were free, there was no cost whatsoever associated with it.

If you wanted to become a doctor, though, you were required to enter a totally different school system after 4th grade, which was a fee-based; and you went on to the university later. So basically, at age 10, you or your parents needed to make that decision and of course have the money to pay for it.

Another option was to enter a *Mittelschule* (junior college) after high school to earn a three-year degree. For us, those schools were in Traunstein, about seven miles away. I went to a Catholic junior college in Traunstein and earned my three-year degree at age 16. There were some bumps in the road, but that's another story.

Chapter 8

The Lesson

It was a day in the spring of 1953. There was still some ice on the streets. We still lived in the building belonging to the Countess Josten in Pfaffing.

A short walk down a gravel road from us was the Klausner farmhouse where we always bought our milk. It was common to buy your milk fresh from the farmer unless you lived in a larger town. We had a tin milk can with a handle. Filled exactly to the bottom of the neck, it held two liters. It was a known fact that, if the farmer's wife filled the can, it was measured just perfectly or a little below because she was a little on the stingy side. The maids were more generous.

Since I was now eight years old, my parents felt I was old enough to be sent to get the milk without my 13-year-old sister Freda having to go with me. This allowed Freda to help mom with other chores.

On my way to the farmer, I was feeling pretty darn proud of myself that my parents had so much confidence in me. So, on the way home, I was kind of happily skipping along, swinging the can a little bit and, oh no, there it was, I tripped and spilled some milk on the street. I felt horrible, how could I have been so irresponsible. I went home, sheepishly put the milk can down. and never said a word about what had happened.

We never went hungry, and mom and dad were trying hard to better our lives. My sister and I knew how hard they had to work to put food on the table. So, when mom looked in the milk can and realized that it was short, I could hear in her voice that she was upset when she asked who had given me the milk. And of course, it happened to have been the farmer's wife. Mom said that Frau Klausner was getting too stingy, and we were no longer going to stand for it. Dad was elected to handle it.

He took the milk can and went on his way to Klausner to address the situation. Halfway there he noticed that there was a spot in the street where the ice was melting. Obviously, it was the spot where I had spilled the milk. He turned around and came back home.

He put down the milk can and, without saying a word, he laid me over his knee and blistered my bottom. He then stood me up, looked me in the eyes and said, "I did not spank you because you spilled the milk, I spanked you because you did not tell the truth." I felt like I was dying inside, I had disappointed my parents; and on top of that I almost let my dad, whom I loved and admired so very much, make a fool of himself with the farmer. What I had done by not owning up to spilling the milk really sunk in.

I learned my lesson well. I knew I had to take responsibility for my actions and accept punishment when needed. And I never lied to my father again. This may also be the reason why I am such a black-and-white person with little tolerance for people telling lies.

Chapter 9

My *Lebensretter* (Lifesaver)

It was 1954, a Saturday shortly after Christmas. School was over at 1 pm, so we were able to enjoy the gorgeous view by daylight. The air was crisp and cold, the snow was like a glistening white blanket, and the view of the Alps was breathtaking.

Herbert and I usually walked home together because Aufham, the village he lived in, was just about one mile past our house. Herbert's family was the poorest family in the area. My mom was best friends with his mom. My mom always had a soft spot for the underdog. She was godmother to all Dangl Resl's children except Herbert. His godfather was the local nursery owner.

On that Saturday we just wanted to enjoy the scenery and not be taunted by some of the kids in school, so we took the back way to our house. Herbert was often teased because of the less than perfect clothes he wore, and I had just gotten glasses that I needed to wear in school and was still being mocked about that.

As we came by the Pletschacher house, the pond was covered with ice. I don't think anyone had ever determined how deep the pond was – or at least we did not know. Herbert stepped on the ice with his rubber boots and everything seemed fine; so I decided I wanted to venture out there as well, except I went out further. The ice started to crackle around my feet and started to break. The water was ice cold, panic hit me, and I was scared to death. I was sure I was going to die!

Being the oldest of a large family, Herbert was used to helping and taking care of others. He knew exactly what to do. He removed some clothing, I don't remember if it was his overalls or his jacket, and while holding onto one side with both hands, threw the other side out to me. I was able just to reach it and hold on for dear life while Herbert pulled me out of the pond.

We just fell into each other's arms shivering, freezing, relieved, but also scared of the consequences I would face from my mom for doing something so stupid. We were about nine years old at the time and had been friends for as long as I can remember. But that day was for sure a day neither one of us would ever forget, and it cemented our friendship for life. I started calling him my *Lebensretter*, which means lifesaver in English. I knew that, when I was with Herbert, I would always be safe.

Our Communion picture is the only one I could find with Herbert and me both in it. I am in the front row, all the way to the left; and Herbert is in the second row, the third one from the left, right by me.

Chapter 10

The Dangl Family

The Dangl Family lived in Aufham, a small village on top of a hill about one kilometer outside Chieming. At that time Chieming and the neighboring small villages accounted for approximately 300 people. That number grew to 500 by 1963 and to 2,000 by 2010.

Aufham was mostly large farms. One of the properties belonged to a well-to-do farmer by the name of Graser. That is where the Dangl family lived. It was an old hut that did not even have indoor plumbing. There was a sign in front of their place that warned you that you are entering at your own risk. Herbert's parents worked for the farmer, and the kids helped in the fields as well. The consensus was that the farmer was majorly taking advantage of the Dangl Family.

Mom and Dangl Resl were best friends and at times shared a cup of mom's coffee on Sunday after church. It was shortly before Resl was going to deliver her baby in 1954 that her husband, Franz, died of a heart attack. Resl already had Herbert, Renate, Hans, Thomas, Peter, and Agnes. The new baby girl, Francisca, made seven. Resl was beside herself trying to figure out how to go on with seven children and no husband; and she consequently suffered a nervous breakdown and was hospitalized.

Herbert went to live with his godfather. My mom, taking her duty as godmother very seriously, took in the other six children including the week-old infant. We had just recently finished building our house in Chieming and were still short some furniture, but we did the best we could.

Almost six months went by, and we finally were informed that Resl was well enough to come home. We had a few days to get her place at the farmer's cleaned up the best we could and get some things in order.

It was a day I will never forget. Church members came to our door to collect for a charity. Dear Lord, I am sure they will never forget that day either. My mom yelled at them at the top of her lungs and the bad language coming out of the mouth could make you blush. She reminded them in no uncertain terms that there was no help offered from the church or anyone else in the six months we were caring for the Dangl children. They had a lot of nerve asking us for help, she said. She also urged them strongly to stock the Dangl place with food and clothes before Resl came home. Food and clothing were abundant and Resl was crying tears of joy when she came home, never knowing what mom had done to make it happen.

Even so it was hard to have six additional people in the family for that long a time; we pulled together, and friendships deepened. Sundays after church was often free time for us kids in the younger years. Down the hill from Herbert's village was a marshy area that we called the jungle. There were mossy areas and little waterways. One had a little wooden float docked on one side where some of the older kids including my sister Freda played Tarzan games. I would look forward to going there with Herbert and his sister Renate. I am sure there were snakes, but I never saw one. Besides, Herbert, my *Lebensretter*, was there with us. We were safe.

You could hear the birds chirping and you could find flowers that only grew there. I remember a little pink flower that was my favorite, we called it Resei, after Herbert's mom and mine. On Mother's Day we would pick some for our mothers.

I always loved happy endings, and the Dangl family story is heartwarming. Once the children had become adults and chose their occupation, they pooled their resources and purchased an old farmhouse in Kraimoos, a village of a few houses halfway between Chieming and Traunstein, the major city in the county. There was a bus stop and of course a *Wirt's* house (tavern).

The family converted the stable and barn to apartments, so each of the children and their families had their own place. Resl maintained the main floor. Herbert's godfather owned the local nursery, and Herbert put the experiences he had gained there to good use. The front yard was spectacular with gorgeous flowers, and the garden in the back was abundant with vegetables and fruits.

Each time I visited my parents in Germany, I made sure I got to visit with Resl and Herbert. I remember a visit in 1980 when my son Scott, age 16, and my daughter Doree, age 12, were with me. Doree came with my mom and me to visit the Dangls. Doree did not speak German. We arrived, and Resl called Herbert to come join us. As soon as he arrived, we hugged and sat down next to each other, we had so much to share. Doree did not understand why we were sitting so close to each other, talking, laughing and hugging. She kept pulling my left hand up showing off my wedding ring. She was trying to remind Herbert and me that I was married. It was so cute.

The Dangl family sold their house many years later, and it became a Bed and Breakfast. Each of the kids used their share of the sale to purchase the home they wanted in the area they had chosen to live in. The last time I saw them was at my mom's funeral in 2005. All the Dangl kids were there to pay mom their last respects, and the priest talked about them living with us for six months.

Even though it was a very sad time, it felt good to reconnect with the Dangl family.

Chapter 11

My Childhood Christmas

Living in the Bavarian Alps on the Austrian border in the 1950s, Christmas was always my favorite time of the year. It was beautiful and peaceful outside. I especially loved the sunsets over the majestic Alps.

Our kitchen was often filled with the wonderful aromas of mom cooking or baking. And there was something soothing about hearing the crackling of the fire in the wood-burning stove there.

A few days before Christmas, dad would go to the forest to select and cut our Christmas tree. He would bring it home and put it in the basement. Mom decorated the tree down there with the most beautiful silver and gold ornaments. She clipped real candles onto the tree, hung a few sparklers, and finished everything off with silver tinsel, being careful to separate the individual strands. This all happened without our seeing a thing.

On Christmas Eve, we would sit down to a supper of bread soup, which is fried bread in broth. It served as a reminder that Mary and Joseph were hungry on Christmas Eve. But mom could even make bread soup taste delicious. Just as we finished eating, mom would get a smirk on her face and disappear. We would then hear some rustling coming from the basement steps and outside the kitchen door.

Soon the Christmas bell would ring. That was our cue to come to the living room. The candles and sparklers were lit, and it was magical. It was so beautiful that it almost felt *holy*. We stood in front of the tree and sang a few Christmas carols, always starting with *"Stille Nacht"* ("Silent Night") and followed by *"O du Froeliche"* ("Oh How Joyful"). I don't know how to describe what it felt like, it was truly special. Christmas Eve was the only time the candles and sparklers were lit, which made that evening even more extraordinary.

Now, we could open our gift. For my sister, Freda, and me, it was always the same – a slip made from sweatshirt material to keep us warm. The only surprise was the color. The slips just came in pink or blue. Still, we were happy and satisfied. Our little brother, Manfred, got a coloring book and color pencils or longjohns when he was older. All of us were already anticipating the treats in store for us the next day.

Pictures of our beautiful Church

Later we went with mom to midnight mass in our beautiful church, but dad stayed home. It was a tradition at Christmas that a family member did that. We called it *Haushuetten,* which meant "watching the house," to make sure nothing bad happened like a fire because everyone used sparklers and real candles on their trees. Dad also made sure the *Wieners* (sausages) were hot and ready when we came home from church cold and hungry.

Christmas always brings back wonderful family memories. Mom started baking early in November and stored the cookies in a cardboard suitcase on top of her closet. When she brought them out on Christmas Day, I swear the cookies tasted fresh baked. Mom always prepared the cookies in a special order. *Lebkuchen* were first, and she used delicious raw honey straight from the beekeeper. After that she made her classic *Spritz* cookies in heart, circle, or cane shapes. Some of them she flavored with finely ground hazelnuts.

Next up were vanilla crescents with a wonderful buttery flavor. Then came star-shaped Linzer cookies, which were classic cookies with a homemade raspberry marmalade filling and a lattice top dusted with confectioners' sugar. Next to *Linzer* cookies, coconut macaroons and hazelnut macaroons were my favorites. Mom would beat the egg whites over hot water on the stove to make sure the cookies would be perfect. My mouth is watering just thinking about those fabulous treats!

On Christmas morning, mom would pull out beautiful Christmas paper plates and fill them with those baked treasures. There was one plate for each of her siblings and her parents, with whom we got together on Christmas Day. Everyone looked forward to mom's cookies and, in turn, brought their treasures for us. It was always something they grew, canned, or made. Uncle Paul always brought walnuts and hazelnuts from his trees. Others brought apples, canned plums or cherries, marmalade, or homemade schnapps.

Everything was abundant and delicious. Mom would make *Gluehwein*, a hot beverage of red wine, cinnamon sticks, cloves, a little sugar, and slices of lemons and oranges. We always had a great time celebrating this joyous season and visiting with family. Christmas was the best time of the year. We were happy, satisfied, and loved.

Chapter 12

Summer Rental

Now that the house was built and my parents no longer had a rent payment, life started to be so much easier financially. With vegetable and meat sources in place, mom was able to cut back a bit on the various jobs she had. Many families in my hometown considered vacation rentals a vital source of income. So, my parents got the necessary furniture for the extra rooms to prepare to offer summer rentals as well.

For one of the rooms, a friend painted used furniture light blue and added the most beautiful flowers. This was the smaller room with a single bed with balcony access which included the breathtaking view of the Alps. It was gorgeous! I was lucky enough to call that my room in the off season.

Mom assigned my sister and me each a room in the basement with a bed, nightstand, and dresser. This is where we slept during the summertime when our rooms were rented out. It was ours to decorate to our heart's desire. At that time, I was very much into movie stars and singers. Some of my favorites were Paul Newman with his baby blues, Alain Delan with his sexy French accent, Horst Buchholz, Romy Schneider, Grace Kelly, Elke Sommer, Doris Day, Pat Boone, Harry Belafonte, and of course my heartthrob Elvis!

My friend Heidi used to subscribe to *Bravo Magazine* and pass the magazines on to me when she was done. I cut out the pictures of my favorites stars and used them as decoration in my basement bedroom. *Bravo Magazine* periodically featured a major star or singer. They would put a picture of part of that individual on the two center pages that measured about 17" x 11". By collecting all the pieces, you would have an almost life-size picture.

When they featured Elvis Presley, I was all in! I could not wait for the next "body part" to complete my idol. Finally, I had all the pieces and promptly glued him on the ceiling over my bed. Elvis was the first thing I saw in the morning. I always woke up in a great mood! In 2004, just before my brother sold the house, Elvis was still smiling down from the ceiling.

Most guest stayed two to four weeks. Breakfast was included in the price of the room. Mom did not skimp. She wanted the guests to feel pampered. Mom or one of us had to pick up fresh-baked "*Broetchen*" (rolls) at the bakery early each morning. When we picked them up, they were still warm and smelled delicious. It was customary to offer fresh coffee, milk, fresh rolls with unsalted butter, ham, cheese, marmalade, and eggs for breakfast. Normally in Germany when you order a cup of coffee, you receive one cup with no refills. Mom spoiled our guests with unlimited refills of her special freshly ground coffee.

We had a book in which guests were asked to write something about their stay. Mom would take a photo of them for the book as well. She would hold a going-away party for them the night before they departed. She made a variety of delicious mini sandwiches cut with a cookie cutter, filled with the best of cheese and ham. Sometimes she would add pinwheels filled with whatever she had on hand.

The platters always looked special and were yummy. There were small pickles cut in half and sliced to look like fans, and of course mom had a signature decoration in the center of the platter. It was a red a mushroom with white dots. In Germany it is called a *Fliegenpilz* and is considered good luck. She made a mushroom stem by cutting a thin scalloped layer of butter with a special knife and rolled it into a stem, then topped it with half a red tomato and dotted it with butter. Mom always took pride in the taste as well as the presentation. The signature drink was pineapple that had been soaked in Schnapps for a several weeks and topped with wine or champagne.

Most of the guests came back year after year. They felt welcome and spoiled. Many booked a year or two in advance. We had three bedrooms for rent, and often guests would bring their friends the next time. As time went on and the children became adults, they would spend their honeymoon and vacations with us.

Often mom had to find additional rooms in the neighborhood as the groups kept growing. We had dozens of books, and guests enjoyed looking at pictures from previous vacations. Herr and Frau Gunst were one of our first guests and came every year after that. They became almost like family. At times Frau Gunst would take me on some fun adventures or just swimming at the lake. Her children were adults, and she did not have grandchildren. Mom was always so busy with outside jobs, taking care of guests, the house, the garden, and us. So sometimes there was just not enough time for everything. Years later, I remember Frau Gunst being the one who took me to buy my first bra.

Below is a picture of Frau Gunst and me in earlier years at the Hirschauer Bucht at Chiemsee. She bought me an inflatable little fish and, judging from the grin on my face, I was having a great time.

In 1955, my sister had just graduated, and Frau Gunst asked Freda what she wanted to do. Her answer was, "Anything, just to get away from here." Freda and mom bumped heads a lot, and Freda wanted to escape. Frau Gunst's daughter, Frau Nierendorf, and her husband owned a restaurant called Jaegerhof in Zweibruecken about 265 miles away. After a short meeting, Freda was hired. The plan was for her to attend trade school and become a chef. Three days later Freda was on the bus to Zweibruecken.

Another special guest was Curt Cuba, a painter from Switzerland. He came at various seasons of the year for solitude and painting. In 1970, Freda and I each received a gift from him. He painted our home in watercolor, dated and signed it for us (in the lower left corner). Mom mailed us the paintings. Below is a picture of the painting.

Chapter 13

My Scary Hospital Stay

When I was in 7th grade in 1958, I ended up in the hospital. The doctors suspected spinal meningitis. I was in isolation with only an infant and a nurse. There was this monstrosity called an iron lung sitting in the corner like a scary monster. I did not know if it was intended for me or the baby. Nevertheless, it scared me to see a huge contraption that only had room for the head to be outside the machine. Every so often someone would come and extract some spinal fluid from me. It was very painful, and I would start crying as soon as I realized what was going to happen.

There was some comfort in having a very caring nurse. Her husband was a teacher, and she had him get school materials for me and helped me study so I would not fall behind. I studied long and hard because that distracted me from thinking about that monstrosity in the corner.

My parents did not have a car, and this hospital was in the Alps. I remember very vividly that they visited me. Because I was in isolation, they could only see me through a small window. I was so happy to see their faces; I had missed them and just wanted to go home with them. Mom was crying and dad was teary-eyed. They brought me two books as a gift. Knowing that it was not easy for my parents to come visit, seeing them cry and bringing me a gift convinced me that I was going to die – and they were just letting me know they loved me before it happened.

After they left, the nurse calmed me down and suggested I read the books they brought, which were *Moby Dick* and *Schatzinsel* (*Treasure Island*). So, for a while I was able to bury myself in the stories and forget my surroundings.

I don't remember how long I was in the hospital, but it seemed like forever. The doctors finally determined that I did not have spinal meningitis, but rather a very bad case of the Asian flu. And after regaining some strength, I was able to return home and resume school.

Chapter 14

Planning for College

It turned out that the studying my nurse had helped me with in the hospital had put me ahead of 7th grade. So at the end of the school year, my favorite teacher, Herr Hager, convinced my parents that it would be the best move for me to skip 8th grade and enroll in junior college. I was praying they would say yes. Knowing they could not afford to pay for my schooling, and that they would not want to give me something they were not able to do for my siblings, I promised to earn the money to pay for school myself. And my parents agreed. I was over the moon!

There were two schools to choose from. One was Sparz, which was a Catholic school with a stellar reputation. Some students lived there, and others were day students. Many Sparz students were promised a job offer in the first year after they would graduate. The second school was co-ed, and it seemed that having fun was more important than studying.

My best friend Heidi was one year older and was planning on going to college as well. We were on the same page about what we wanted to achieve. I was so glad to be able to share this next adventure with Heidi, and it also was comforting for both of us to know we would be able to support each other in tackling the many unknowns going forward as we enrolled in Sparz.

Tuition for Heidi was not an issue. She was an only child, and her parents were well off. But I needed to get on the ball and determine my costs so I could properly plan. Besides tuition, I would need bus fare. I could bring that cost down by only planning on using the bus during the winter months and rainy days and then bicycling the rest of the time for the six miles each way. My Goed (Godfather) who was also my Onkel Hans, whom I loved very much, was the local milk truck driver. He offered to pick me up early in the morning on rainy days, take me on his rounds to the various farmers, and drop me off at school because the end of his route was close to Sparz. This way I could save a one-way bus fare on those days and would just have to get up very early.

In addition, I had a wonderful surprise coming when Mom and Dad again did something very much out of the ordinary and bought me a typewriter, which I desperately needed. I understood that the typewriter was to be my birthday and Christmas presents for the next three years.

Job hunting was easy as my parents had a reputation for being honest and hardworking, and the assumption was that I would be as well. I secured a job bussing tables for Fuechserl (my favorite teacher's wife) at Oberwirt. She was very flexible with my schedule so I could work at the lake as well.

We had two facilities at the lake with different owners. The Bad was a place where you rented a small changing room. They had outside tables to serve sandwiches, snacks, drinks, candy, and ice cream. Lounges and umbrellas were also for rent. I worked for Chemo Bad. The owner came only in the summer. He paid me for the first month and told me that he would pay me at the end of the season to see if he could give me a good bonus. I felt that, if I would get more money, I would somehow manage until the end of the season. But when we got the first end-of-summer storm, he closed, left town, and never paid me.

I was devastated! I needed that money. To help me out, mom let me take over one of her jobs, Herr Hartinger, who lived in a small apartment above Tante Marie's café. He was partially paralyzed, and besides shopping he needed a variety of daily things done. His wife had moved to Chicago to be with her daughter. The reason why she chose to move to America and leave him behind, I don't know. He was such a dear man, and I felt so badly for him.

To help mom out for letting me have one of her jobs that fit into my schedule, I helped her by cleaning the post office and phone booth every day. In the end, it all worked out.

Chapter 15

My First Year of College

Sparz, Traunstein

During registration, local business owners came to Sparz, interviewed new students, and determined if they were interested in hiring them after graduation. Many job offers were made at that point, which ensured that students would receive any specialty classes they needed for their upcoming jobs. I was lucky enough to secure a job with the owner of Kaufhaus Unterforsthuber, the largest department store in the county. Shorthand was the only additional skill the owner required.

Studying was never a huge chore for me. So I was fine until about two months into the first year, when I realized that English did not come that easy for me and I needed to go back to square one. I approached Fraulein English, my English teacher and explained my situation. I told her I would catch up as quickly as possible but also needed to keep up my jobs to pay for school. Her answer was that my family was not from the desired social class, and I should consider leaving Sparz. Fraulein English refused to give me a chance to catch up, and instead had me take a test every day while she was teaching the rest of the class.

I was at my wit's end and needed someone to talk to. Matter Walburga, my shorthand teacher, was very caring and approachable. I shared my dilemma and tearfully explained my situation and asked for advice. She was aware that I was going to work for Unterforsthuber and knew that English was not required for that job. Her advice was to do the best I could; and she assured me that, as long as I kept my grades up to 1s and 2s and only had one 5 (the grading scale went from 1 to 6 instead of A to F), I would be able to graduate. Matter Walburga would periodically check up on me and give me encouragement. I found out later that she also made Matter Jutta, the principal, aware of my dilemma. They both became my favorite nuns at Sparz.

Shortly thereafter dad had a horrible accident with a lengthy hospital stay. Matter Jutta came to my rescue by allowing me to do my afternoon studies by my father's bedside. I will tell you more about this later.

When riding the bus, Heidi and I had plenty of time to visit or study together. Anneliese, another student at Sparz, joined us at the next bus stop; and the three of us became close. On sunny days Anneliese and I would meet up and ride our bicycles to school together. The challenge was the Erlstaetter Berg, a hill about one mile long. We would encourage each other all the way up, trying not to have to push the bike, and many times we made it!

The three of us became good friends with two classmates, Gisela and Ilse. They were half-sisters and were born 11 months apart. Ilse, the youngest, was conceived in one of Hitler's "breeding houses." Under Hitler's orders, Aryan-looking women were impregnated by Aryan men to produced racially pure children. At one point even married women, as happened in Ilse's mother's case, were forced into this program and impregnated by Aryan SS officers. Once a child was born, it was to be turned over to an SS family to be raised. Ilse was supposed to be blond and blue-eyed, but she had brown hair and brown eyes. Luckily, she was born after the war was over, or her fate could have been death. It was hard to comprehend such unspeakable acts. Gisela shared that her dad accepted his wife's child, Ilse, as his own and loved her as his daughter. By the grace of God, the family was whole!

Chapter 16

My 14th Birthday

It was 1959, and I was celebrating my 14th birthday. I felt I would have graduated high school and could be on my own if I had not chosen to go to college. So consequently, I should not have as many social restrictions as my mother had placed on me. On that day, September 12, 1959, the Red Cross was putting on a show at the lake, and mom allowed me to go with the understanding I would be home by 7 pm.

I put on my most prized possession, a light blue tiered skirt with beautiful flowers and an eyelet edge that I had received from Herr Hartinger's wife in America. I felt grown up and pretty, and I had such a great time. I met a guy named Guenther who had just come to town with a crew that was looking for oil drilling locations, and the crew planned to stay in Chieming for several months.

I heard the church bell announce 7 o'clock, and I was still at the lake and frankly did not care. About 30 minutes later, the two of us started to take the back way to our house. Guenther was pushing my bike, and we talked and talked. He lived near Hamburg, in the very northern part of Germany, and I was fascinated by his stories.

It was probably close to 8 pm when I got home. Mom's cousin Fanny was in the kitchen and asked where I had been. She said mom had been looking for me and was so worried, with all these strangers in town, that she went to the police to ask for their help in finding me. I knew I was in trouble. I told Fanny I was going to come up with an excuse and begged her not let on that I was not being truthful. Fanny agreed.

I went outside, took the chain of my three-speed bike, and smeared the grease all over my skirt and me. I went to the police station, let mom know how sorry I was that I worried her, but said I had had bike issues and had ruined my favorite skirt. Mom's cousin never said anything. However, I lived in a small town. Several people had seen me with Guenther and told mom the next day. There was definitely a punishment not easily forgotten. I head learned my lesson as an eight-year-old not to lie and to take responsibility for my actions. This incident drove it home one more time in a big way!

Chapter 17

Oktoberfest

When I grew up, one of the festivities we all looked forward to was the *Oktoberfest*. It was a celebration bursting with music, dancing, laughter, camaraderie, and of course bratwurst. I loved it all. As for the food, I mostly looked forward to the side dishes: potato salad with hot bacon dressing, sauerkraut seasoned with bacon and simmered in a combination of white wine and broth, sweet and sour red cabbage, pretzels, and salads in many colors.

Bavarians are known for their "*Salatplatte*," a colorful array of at least four different salads on a bed of butter lettuce. We always added white radish salad because that was dad's favorite plus pickled pumpkin like Oma used to make. Once we were so stuffed that we thought we could not eat another bite, the desserts came out. Anything from *Apfelstrudel* to plum cake with whipped cream, Black Forest Cherry Cake, and a delicate cheesecake along with various pastries. Of course, we could not pass that up. Let me share with you the radish salad dad liked so much:

White Radish Salad

1 large white Daikon radish
2 teaspoons salt
1/3 teaspoon sugar
1 tablespoon white vinegar
1 rounded tablespoon sour cream
unwhipped whipping cream

Peel and grate radish, then mix with about 2 teaspoons of salt and let it soak for 30 minutes.

Squeeze until almost dry, then add sugar and white vinegar, sour cream, and unwhipped whipping cream to get desired texture and taste.

In case you are curious how the *Oktoberfest* started, let me tell you the story. Bavarians are grateful to Prince Ludwig I and Princess Therese for starting this tradition over 200 years ago. Its origin goes back to October 12, 1810, the wedding day of Bavaria's Prince Ludwig, who later became King Ludwig I, and Princess Therese. The Bavarian royalty did the unheard of by inviting the citizens of Munich to the wedding. Some 40,000 people showed up for the celebration on the fields in front of the city gates, which is called Theresen Wiesen or now simply called the *Wies'n*.

It appears the royal couple selected the date to coincide with the annual depletion of the last beer from the spring to make room for the new brew. Before refrigeration, brewers found the beers they made in the summer tended to have undesirable "off" flavors and aromas. Consequently, Germany instituted a rule which forbade the production of beer during the warmer months. This meant the beers brewed in the spring had to carry them through the non-brewing months.

I always wondered why the royal couple chose the end of the brewing moratorium for their wedding day. Did they just have a lot of beer to get rid of, and that's why they invited the whole town? Regardless, the reception was so much fun that no one wanted to stop; and the party continued for 16 days.

A year later, the citizens of Munich decided to throw the party all over again as an anniversary tribute to the royal couple. It was such a successful event that it became an annual tradition that was canceled only in times of war or disease.

Today, *Oktoberfest* is a fall celebration of good beer, good food, good friends, and good times. There are horseracing tournaments among many other festivities and contests. *Oktoberfest* is known to be the largest beer festival in the world. Just to give you an idea, in 2019 Munich was visited by 6.3 million people for the festival; and 7.3 million liters of beer were consumed in addition to roughly 95,000 liters of wine and 43,000 liters of champagne.

In case you are wondering why it is called *Oktoberfest*, yet it starts in September; I will tell you. In 2010 the dates were changed to make sure it stays warmer in the evening and daylight is long enough to enjoy the festivities. It is still 16 days, but now it starts in September and always ends the first weekend in October. And that's why the *Oktoberfest* dates change.

Each year, the mayor of Munich personally taps the first keg of Spaten beer to open the *Oktoberfest*, crowning the deed with a big "*O'zaft is*" (it's tapped). That marks the beginning of the festival.

| Mal & Ron | Freda and I serving Cake | Debby & Ron Hart |

My husband Mal, my sister Freda, and I have frequently held an *Oktoberfest* for family and friends. We shared the tradition with eight friends in 2013. The word spread, and more and more people wanted to come. In 2018 we had over 100 people celebrate with us. To accommodate that many people in our backyard, we had to split the celebration into two days.

Our preparations start a few days in advance. Bratwurst and beer get ordered. Mal makes sure tables and Bavarian decorations are set up, and the props for picture-taking are in the right spots. Debby and Ron join him to help. I plan the food and write out the *Speisekarte* (menu) and make sure I have all the fixings for authentic German food. I make pickled pumpkin a few days before, to make sure it absorbs all the spices. Freda comes the day before and makes her famous Black Forest Cherry Cakes. The rest gets prepared the morning of the *Oktoberfest*.

Freda's famous Black Forest Cherry Cake

Batter:
6 egg yolks
1 cup sugar (divided)
1 pkg. Oetker vanilla sugar or a cap of vanilla
2 tablespoons hot water
1 bottle Oetker rum extract or a capful of rum flavoring
6 egg whites
½ cup all-purpose flour
¼ cup cocoa
3 tablespoons corn starch
1 teaspoon baking powder
Kirsch or Brandy, optional

For the Filling:

2 cups heavy whipping cream
3 tablespoons sifted powdered sugar
2 pkg. Oetker vanilla sugar or 2 caps vanilla extract
1 ½ cups cherry pie filling
3 squares semi-sweet chocolate grated or
chocolate sprinkles
maraschino cherries for decoration

Preheat oven to 350.

Grease and flower a 9½ inch spring form, line bottom with parchment paper.

Beat egg yolks, 2/3 cups of the sugar, vanilla, hot water, and rum essence until thick and creamy.

Beat egg whites with remaining 1/3 cup sugar to stiff peaks.

Sift flour, cocoa, cornstarch, and baking powder together and gently fold into the egg yolk mixture.

Fold egg whites in and pour in pan.

Bake for 45 to 50 minutes until toothpick inserted in center comes out clean.

Remove from pan immediately, turn onto a cake platter, remove wax paper, and cool the cake.

Slice cake in half to make two layers. Drizzle bottom with Kirsch or brandy if desired.

Whip cream to soft peaks; gradually add powdered sugar, and vanilla; and beat to stiff peaks.

Spread cherry pie filling on bottom cake layer.

Spread 1/3 of the cream mixture on top of the pie filling and add top layer of the cake.

Spread cream on the sides of the cake reserving a little for decoration.

Cover sides and top with grated chocolate.

Decorate top with whipped cream dollops and cherries.

Once all the guests have arrived, I start the festivities with the story of the origin of the festival and a hardy *Prost*!

Of course, we have Spaten beer, wine, and *Radler. Radler* (bicyclist) is a mixture of beer and 7Up. Yes, many said "yuck!" the first time they heard it but, once they tried it, it became the most requested beverage at the *Oktoberfest. Radler* came about in Germany because the beer there has a higher alcohol level. On a warm day, bicyclists were looking forward to a nice cool beer at their rest stop but wanted or needed more than one glass to cool down and socialize. Hence, *Radler* was invented and is on the menu in most Bavarian restaurants.

Mal and his buddy Ron, both in Lederhosen of course, grill the brats, fresh from Mattern Sausage in Orange, a family-owned German butcher who emigrated from Rosenheim, Germany, a long time ago. Debby, Freda, and I, wearing Bavarian dresses, offer dessert along with coffee, followed by various kinds of schnapps.

Mal enjoys taking pictures of our friends with the Bavarian Gal and Guy props as a remembrance. Debby and Ron take videos and candid shots throughout the celebration. The following year we stream the videos and pictures on TV for everyone's enjoyment. All the photos from the previous year are posted on a board and available for guests to take home as a memento.

It has always been a heartwarming and special experience for my sister and me to be able to share and celebrate our heritage with our family and friends.

Chapter 18

A Life-Changing Tragedy

One of the spring highlights in our town was the *Maibaum* (Maypole) celebration. The maypole tradition is a very popular ritual in Bavaria and parts of Austria. This custom dates to the 18th century when people danced around certain trees in hopes of harvesting large crops.

Each March the maypole from the previous year is removed to make room for the new one to be erected on May 1. Preparations start in the barn of one of the farmers. The right size tree is selected and cut down, and its branches are removed and cleared so that only a clean log is left. The pole is wrapped with fresh green garlands and blue-and-white ribbons. Next, carved or painted signs are attached for each type of trade or industry in the village. Everyone visiting or driving through town can tell from looking at the maypole if there is a shoemaker, blacksmith, furniture maker, painter, brewery, butcher shop, etc., in the village.

On May 1, the youngest dancer group in full costume gets to sit on the horse-drawn wagon with the maypole as it makes its way down the town's main street. The local band accompanied by the rest of the dancing groups in traditional clothes lead the way. Once the destination is reached, the guys in lederhosen raise the maypole. The dancers weave the blue-and-white streamers back and forth in a fashion to create the Bavarian flag pattern.

There is music, dancing, laughing, plenty of food and beer but, most important, great camaraderie. It's a celebration everyone looks forward to.

So it was that on April 30, 1959, that dad was looking forward to enjoying the maypole celebration. He had been on his motorcycle for close to six hours coming home for the first time in a month from a construction job in Bad Toelz. It was about 11 pm and he was now less than a ½ mile from home. The main street in Chieming was a single lane on each side. Dad was behind three young women who were riding on their bicycles next to each other taking up the entire lane. Dad honked a couple of times, but they would not move. So, he decided to go around them which put him right at the center line.

At the same time, the butcher from Unterwirt was coming the opposite way. He was rather intoxicated. And he, too, was right on the center line. As fate would have it, the left front fender of the butcher's Mercedes caught dad's left knee and twisted his leg backwards over the saddlebags on the back of the motorcycle, which were holding his belongings. The girls took off, and the butcher pulled over to the side and passed out.

Dad was lying on the ground bleeding while the motorcycle was still running. Dad pulled his belt off and made a tourniquet for his leg, but that's all he could do; he was helpless otherwise. Max and his brother Bernhard, dad's closest friends, were on their way home from the same rehearsal the girls had attended. Max and Bernhard came to dad's aid, summoning an ambulance and the police. The police officer who responded was the brother of the intoxicated butcher, who was still passed out on the side of the road.

The ambulance took dad to the hospital in Traunstein, about six miles away. On that fateful night, three major accidents had happened and only one surgeon was available at the hospital. Six breaks were found on dad's left leg. For some reason they determined they needed to amputate his leg. It was later determined that there was an additional break in the hip that they did not identify, which eliminated the possibility that dad could wear a functional prosthesis. There were other issues with the surgery, but I don't know the details.

At the time I was going to college in Traunstein. The principal, Matter Jutta, came to my aid once more and gave me permission to spend my afternoons by my dad's bedside instead of at the school. I was able to see him almost daily for those first few months at the hospital. Sometimes dad would sleep, other times we would talk a little, but most of the time it was just the comfort of being there together.

Dad ended up spending almost one and a half years hospitalized, several months in Traunstein and later in a rehabilitation hospital in Murnau. We did not have a car, and there was no bus line to Murnau. This was a very difficult time for our family. We were dependent on someone with a car to take us to visit dad and, because we did not have a phone, we could not even call him.

This horrible accident affected so many lives. Dad was only 49 years old, and now his dreams were shattered. He had fantasized of seeing more of the world. Dad was so honored when he was selected to go with his employer to Australia for one year to build houses. This assignment was to start at the end of May. Dad was looking forward to being able to provide especially well for his family upon his return. But now, financial security and enjoyments like activities with his family, dancing, riding his motorcycle, nature walks, performing in the local theater – all these had disappeared. But dad never complained, that just was not in his nature.

The financial impact of the loss of dad's income was tremendous. Mom tried to make up for it by taking on even more jobs. There was very little time left for her to relax and do the things she wanted or liked doing. She worried a lot about dad and probably wondered what life would be like going forward. I am sure she also thought about all the activities and fun dad and she would now be missing out on. I sometimes could hear mom cry softly at night. But she never complained, she just did what needed to be done.

We all tried to deal with the situation in our own way. My sister was not home; she needed to continue her career in northern Germany. I tried to juggle school, work, and being with dad. Mom took care of our physical needs, and she worried about all of us and, of course, finances. My brother was eight years old and found himself being alone a lot. He started acting like a brat sometimes and got into some trouble that continued even into his teenage years. For almost one and a half years, dad was not there to guide my brother; and we were all trying to do the best we could. In retrospect, I wonder if I could not have carved out more time for my brother.

April 30, 1959, was indeed a life-changing tragedy!

Chapter 19

Graduation and the Next Step

Between school, work, chores, and dad, the next two years just flew. Heidi, Anneliese, Gisela, and Ilse were pretty much the group I enjoyed spending time with. We had worked hard for our degree, and finally the big day had arrived!

Graduation time! There were no big festivities planned, it just was not the custom. Finishing what you started was an expectation. However, the five of us decided to celebrate our accomplishments at the ice cream specialty café in the town center and indulge in an *Eisbecher*, which is ice cream served in a beautifully shaped glass with sinfully delicious toppings of your choice.

Our future was secure as all five of us had a job waiting for us. We savored our *Eisbecher*, reminisced about the last three years, and shared our visions of the future. We got teary-eyed saying our goodbyes and promised to stay in touch. We were now ready and eager to start the next chapter.

I had only one week to get ready for my job at Unterforsthuber. The owner with whom I had interviewed three years earlier had retired, and the daughter had taken over the business. She was not the lady her mother was! She lacked people skills, and she was abrupt and abrasive. The job was not what had been proposed to me, and the pay was, to put it mildly – lousy!

I tried to share with the new owner what her mother and I had discussed regarding job responsibilities and let her know the salary was not what I had been led to believe. Her response was basically that she makes the decisions now, not her mother, then handed me a chocolate bar. Really??

Discouraged, I shared this with my mother. Just then our neighbor, Herr Putz, came to make his monthly payment for the garage he rented from us. After hearing what had transpired at my job, he strongly encouraged me to apply for a position at Siemens in Traunreut where he worked. He felt that I would fit into several jobs there and told me just to take anything to get my foot in the door, as he was certain great opportunities would open for me. He was willing to let me ride-share with him in exchange for the garage rent.

Siemens had one job open at the time, which was a librarian at two and a half times the salary I was making at Unterforsthuber. I applied for the position, went for the interview, and was hired. However, I was told the job was not open for three more months, but they could temporarily place me in another department until that time if I was interested.

When I gave my notice to Frau Unterforsthuber, suddenly, she was willing to change my job responsibilities and salary to coincide with what her mother had discussed with me. However, that did not sway my decision. So, in August 1961, I officially started at Siemens.

Traunreut was a huge plant that made all sorts of appliances from toasters to refrigerators, washing machines, etc. In addition to local employees, Siemens also hired workers from Italy and Greece.

The function of the department I was temporary working in was to calculate the time allowed for making and assembling parts plus projecting the cost for each appliance. Calculations about adjustments that would save time and costs were also done there. Accuracy was extremely important as errors could affect jobs and appliance costs. I was trained on a special machine called SumLock, which was imported from England. Calculators were not invented until six years later in 1967. I learned the machine and routine quickly and loved what I was doing. By the way, a SumLock machine is now displayed in the National Museum of American History. Boy, does that make me feel old!

There were 21 men of various ages in our department who timed different tasks on the assembly line. The information was than provided to me and Traudl, a young lady a year older than me, to perform the calculations. I love working with numbers, and I was in my element. Within six months, I was promoted to Officer and stayed there until I got married and moved to America. Needless to say, I never made it to the library.

Just a few little funny stories about that time. Traudl and I had a lot in common and got along well. Both of us came from strict families. Make-up was frowned on by our parents. But we were young and had other ideas. At lunch we would sometimes read ads in magazines about all sorts of wonderful things. A couple of items in particular caught our interest. One was something to put on your lips to make them "irresistible," the other one was a cream to increase your bust size. Who would not want irresistible, kissable lips? And since both of us weighed just over 100 pounds and were rather flat-chested, increasing our bust size was a dream come true.

We decided that these two items were exactly what we needed. We skipped lunches for a couple of weeks and used the money to buy those two wonderful products. We were so excited when the package arrived at work. So as soon as we got to work the next morning, we applied the magic lip treatment and waited for the super potion to dry, only to find out it was like clear nail polish. Once we moved our lips, it cracked and hurt to remove. Bummer!

Well, all was not lost yet – the magical jar that was going to give us those big boobs we both wanted so badly was the next thing. It was a jar with a green cream that needed to be massaged onto the breast twice daily. Which we did diligently! After one week of that, I was approached by Herr Fritzenwanger, the youngest and best looking of the 21 men in the department. He had been charged by his coworkers to let us know that the new perfume Traudl and I were using smelled horrible, and he asked that we please stop using it. It was our green bust cream. So that was the end of that adventure!

I stayed with Siemens until the end of 1962. Herr Lensch, my boss, wrote me a wonderful letter of reference. He also told me to just let him know if America did not work out for me. They would love to have me back.

Siemens was an excellent company to work for! How lucky was I to have had such a wonderful experience as my first real job!

Chapter 20

Mom's Family

Egerer Oma and Opa

Mom's parents, Egerer Oma and Opa, got married on May 5, 1912, and had five children. They lived in Egerer, a small village on the outskirts of Chieming.

This is their wedding picture.

Funny little tidbit here. I asked mom if she could please find a wedding picture of her parents. She managed to find one. However, when I got this picture, to help us identify family members, mom had marked her mother's family with dots on the chin and her dad's family with dots on the forehead. Freda and I still laugh about that.

Mom's childhood home was a big farmhouse in Egerer with many fruit trees. There were cows, chickens, pigs, doves, and one horse. There were cherry, apple, and pear trees in addition to walnut trees and hazelnut bushes.

Oma always had lots of laundry; and it seemed like every day of the week, except on Sundays, clothes were drying on the line in the sun. For a long time, there was no indoor plumbing. We had to use an outhouse that had a heart cutout on the door. I hated the cut newspaper that served as TP and was hung on something like a very big safety pin.

Egerer Oma   *Egerer Opa*

Oma

Mutti's mother was Therese Kendler (known as Guetlermutter); but to Freda, Manfred, and me, she was Egerer Oma. She was one of 24 children of which 14 lived. Back then, no allowances were made if you were pregnant, you had the same responsibilities as non-pregnant women. I assume that was the reason for a lot of still births. Oma was born on Friday, October 14, 1881, in Unterwendling by St. Leonhart in Bavaria. Her maiden name was Maier. She died the day before my ninth birthday at age 73 of liver cancer.

Oma had a huge garden full of vegetables and lots of lettuce. She had a pumpkin patch and, in the fall, she made the best sweet-and-sour pickled pumpkin. Freda and I still make and love it. I would like to share that recipe with you:

Sweet and Sour Pumpkin

1 pie pumpkin, peeled and seeded, cut into 1inch cubes
1½ to 2 cups sugar – depending how sweet you want it
2½ cup white wine vinegar
¼ to ½ cup water
1 lemon – juice and grated rind
2- to 3-inch stick peeled ginger
2 cinnamon sticks
6 cloves

Place the pumpkin in a large, deep bowl.

In a large saucepan, mix everything except pumpkin. Boil 5 minutes. Pour the hot liquid over the pumpkin in the bowl. Cover and set aside 8 hours, or overnight.

Remove the cinnamon sticks, ginger and cloves. Place everything in a pot and boil until pumpkin is transparent but crisp, about

15 minutes or so. Allow the mixture to cool. Transfer to sterile jars and refrigerate.

Oma also grew a variety of beautiful flowers. One side of the garden was edged with huge sunflowers. In the middle, I remember her beautiful bleeding hearts surrounded by forget-me-nots. Both are still some of my favorite flowers.

I don't remember Oma ever talking or smiling, and she always wore black dresses and grey aprons with very narrow white stripes on them. I think she never got over her son Sepp's being killed in the war in Russia. My mom shared that Oma claimed Sepp came to see her in her sleep the day he died. When she told the rest of the family about it in the morning, nobody believed her and thought she was just worried about him until they received notification several weeks later that he had died that night. Oma obviously had some sort of vision or feeling. His death hit her hard. Freda and I believe that's why Oma never talked much after that and always wore black or grey. I sometimes wondered if she planted the bleeding hearts and the forget-me-nots in her garden in memory of her child.

I can't even remember Oma's voice. But there was never a question about her love. Her actions spoke louder than words. Egerer Oma used to churn butter and shape it into round one-pound loaves. To give it her signature touch, she used a spoon to make the top look like a rose. Her butter was beautiful! The butter was sold, and the family ate margarine or lard. I remember her lard and salt sandwiches on fresh baked rye bread. I actually enjoyed them.

Oma made the butter in what was called a *Butterfass* (butter churner). The churner looked like a narrow round wood barrel with a pole inserted through the lid of the churn. She would move the handle up and down until the butter was done. If she was churning butter when we visited, she would pull me next to her and, as she churned, she would pull the churner higher than usual and make sure it scraped against the side, so a little butter would accumulate on top. She would guide my finger to wipe that butter for me to eat. Those were some of the ways she showed me her love. Sweet unsalted butter will always be my favorite.

I was just nine years old when she died. I remember being very upset with my Opa at the funeral and then the wake because he was not crying like I was. I did not understand he probably was celebrating her life. I just knew I was hurting, missed her tremendously, and expected everyone else to feel and express it the same way. Following is a picture of happier times when the family was still all together.

Back row – Hans, Paul, Sepp, Marie & Resi.
Front Row – Egerer Opa and Egerer Oma

Opa

Mutti's father was Johann Kendler (known as Guetlervater); but to Freda, Manfred, and me, he was Egerer Opa. He was one of 17 children of which 13 lived. He was born on Sunday, July 27, 1884, in Obermosen by St. Leonhart in Bavaria. He died at age 80 of stomach cancer, a year after I came to America. I was never close to him. Sometimes I wondered why Oma married him, and then I realized that she was 31 years old when she entered into an arranged marriage.

Mom never shared a lot about her relationship with her dad. When I saw how he treated her compared to her sister Marie, it was clear whom he liked better. Mom wore glasses with very thick lenses. When I was eight years old and got my glasses, I was a little worried that my vision would get as bad as hers; so I asked her when she got her glasses. She told me that she was about my age when her eyes got bad very quickly. She shared that, one day when she stepped up on the bench in the kitchen to see what time it was, Opa felt she had just developed a stupid habit and did not believe she had a problem. He threatened to spank her if she continued to pretend. A few months went by and Opa was finally contacted by the school about mom's vision problem. The school told him to get mom's eyes checked. Reluctantly they took her to see the doctor, and it was determined that she had an infection in the lining of the brain which caused the vision issue. Even though the infection was treated, the damage to her eyes was irreversible.

On the day mom went into labor on March 9, 1951, Dad made a bet with Opa that it was going to be a boy. Opa only had granddaughters to that point. And as it turned out, mom gave birth to my brother, Manfred. Opa was convinced dad was not telling the truth. Opa said he would not believe it or pay up until he could make a personal inspection.

Opa had his favorites and Freda, Manfred, and I were not it. It seems that the only time he was nice to us was when the cherries were ripe. He would allow us to climb up in the cherry trees and eat to our heart's content. The first thing Freda and I did was to look for two perfect cherry pairs each and hang them on our ears like earrings.

I remember two of Opa's sisters. Great-aunt Hedwig lived close by in Siegsdorf and came to visit often. She looked a lot like Opa but was a lot nicer. Great-aunt Amalie married a gypsy. They finally settled on a piece of land in a remote area. I remember the big and bountiful vegetable garden. The main house had a bedroom and large kitchen. There was an outhouse, a well, and a variety of little huts they seemed to have added as needed.

Aunt Amalie was called a psychic, and she seemed to really have a gift. People came to her when they were troubled to get advice or just to find out what life had in store for them. Mom took me to visit there a few times. One time, when I was 14, my great-aunt was very insistent that I needed to stay away from my girlfriend with the short dark hair, as there was trouble brewing. That friend was Brigitte. She was a year older than me, was very beautiful, and was often left alone. Mom forbid me to see her, and I was very angry. It turned out shortly after that warning from my great-aunt that Brigitte got pregnant by a married man. It was the town scandal.

When Opa died, he left the farm and the surrounding acreage to Onkel Paul. I don't know what Goed and Tante Marie received, I just know my mom received nothing.

Onkel Hans Kendler

Mom's younger brother was Hans. He was born on Wednesday, October 14, 1914. To Freda, Manfred, and me, he was Goed

(Godfather). Being Goed is more important than uncle. An uncle or an aunt are relatives; however, your godparents have been chosen to take care of you in case your parents can't.

Goed always had a smile on his face. I loved him very much and always enjoyed the time we could spend together. He was the local milk truck driver, which meant that he picked up the milk from the farmers and delivered it to the dairy. His route took him through various villages, large and small. He knew all the side roads and had a great relationship with all the farmers. Goed had a lot of patience and never rushed the farmers if they ran a little late. Many of those farmers still had baking huts to bake large amounts of bread. They appreciated Goed and frequently gave him fresh baked bread or cheese, potatoes, fruits, and vegetables.

Goed was married to Maria who was born in December 1915. They built a beautiful home in Chieming near the lake. She was also Gon (Godmother) to Freda, Manfred, and me. In turn mom was godmother to all three of their daughters, Antonia, Marita, and Christa. Sometimes Gon and Goed would take me with them to pick wild blueberries in the Alps. I loved the taste of those fresh, just-picked, juicy blueberries and would fill my tummy with those little delicacies. And I would come home with a blue tongue.

My cousin Marita, the middle one, was the one I always liked the best. She was married to Koni (Konrad), the love of her life. They had one daughter, Isolde, and two boys, Wolfi and Konrad. When the children were still very small, Koni died in a car accident. Marita never remarried and still lives in the same house that looks like an old castle in Chieming.

I always thought of my Goed as this good-hearted, tall, strong guy with a winning smile. He loved the Alps and loved going mountain climbing with his buddies.

The guy on top is my Goed.

In his 60s, he developed stomach cancer and had part of his stomach removed. He had to make some major adjustments but continued enjoying life and never lost that captivating smile of his.

When I went on my first visit in many years to Germany and visited Goed, he did not seem so tall anymore. But he still had all the qualities that I treasured about him.

In 1980 Freda and I took her daughter Carola and my son Scott and daughter Doree on a trip to Germany. On that visit, Goed asked us to put a day aside for him as he had a surprise planned. The surprise was to take all of us to the blueberry hill, the same place he used to take me to as a child. We were so lucky that we picked the right time to make that visit as the blueberries were abundant.

What a fabulous day we had. We are out there in the fresh mountain air, enjoying those sweet, justpicked blueberries. And of course I was reliving some treasured childhood memories. It was special to be able to share that experience with my sister, children, and my niece.

Funny thing, we all came back with blue tongues, just like when I was a child.

Onkel Sepp Kendler

Joseph (Sepp) was born on Wednesday, January 2, 1918. I don't know a lot about him. Mom told me that he was in a serious relationship, I don't know her name. Sepp wanted to wait to get married until he got back from the war. He was deployed to Russia, where he was killed on Wednesday, May 5, 1943, on his parents' 31st wedding anniversary. His death hit Oma pretty hard, and she was never the same after that.

I have very view pictures of Sepp. One is the portrait of him as a small child with Oma, Mutti, and Goed in Mutti's story. He is in a family picture in Oma's story, and the third one I have is with his girlfriend below.

His name is on the memorial of fallen soldiers at the church in Chieming.

The Twins – Onkel Paul and Tante Marie

Tante Marie and Onkel Paul

Maria Selbertinger (Tante Marie)

Maria, whom we lovingly called Tante Marie, was twin to Onkel Paul. They were born on Saturday, March 6, 1920. In 1943 Tante Marie gave birth to her daughter, Marianne, I believe by a soldier who never returned from the war. In 1949 she married Hans, a pastry chef. Onkel Hans and Tante Marie leased a property on the main street in Chieming and opened a café and a pastry bakery.

My mouth waters as I think about all the scrumptious pastries and cakes Onkel Hans made. The *Obst Torte* (fancy fresh fruit tart), *Erdbeer Sahne Torte* (strawberry cream torte) and *Zwetschgen Datschi* (fresh plum cake) were among my favorites. I also loved the chocolate-dipped *Spritz* pastries made with marzipan. Onkel Hans did the baking, and Tante Marie took care of the café and the sales in the pastry shop.

In 1951 they welcomed a baby girl, Lisbeth, into the family. Even though he was not Marianne's biological father, Onkel Hans always treated the two girls equally. There was never a question about his love for both.

Freda spent a lot of time at the café and pastry shop. She had a fantastic relationship with Tante Marie, and she was closer to her than our mom. Frequently she helped Onkel Hans baking and cleaning up. She never said it out loud, but I bet she loved licking the bowls.

Tante Marie had worked at the post office and was trained in projecting a professional image. She had a flair about her which made her such a perfect owner of a café. She had this special decorating talent and an amazing sense of color coordination. Her Christmas tree was always spectacular. She changed the décor annually.

Mom would help at the café and pastry shop but in a domestic fashion, such as cleaning, ironing, etc. So the relationship between Tante Marie and mom at times appeared as if mom was not as good as Tante Marie. Opa always seemed to be at the café as well, which did not help matters. I could sense that mom felt inferior, but that did not stop her from bringing strawberries and eggs to Tante Marie for the baked goods. After all, they were sisters.

Onkel Hans always had a smile on his face. He organized and led the *Fasching* (*Karneval*) parade for the children. He would help us with the *Fasching* makeup and costumes. Onkel Hans was adored by all of us children. Sadly, he died in 1973 of cancer.

Tante Marie lit a candle on Onkel Hans' grave every day until she no longer could make it to the grave. Her daughters would then take her once a week. His picture was on her living room wall until she died 35 years after him. Truly a special love! You will note that, in her wedding picture, she is not wearing a white veil. That is because she had a child out of wedlock before she married Hans and a white veil would not have been appropriate.

After the café was sold, Tante Marie lived in the house next to Lisbeth and in Marianne's house upstairs. Tante Marie was able to enjoy afternoon coffee with both her daughters every day. Freda and I still call that "playing Tante Marie" when we have the opportunity to have coffee together.

Tante Marie would not share her special recipes. She would always make *Obst Torte* or *Erdbeer Sahne Torte* for us when we visited. So, on one of our visits to Germany, Freda and I asked her to please share those two recipes. She finally agreed and told us to be there the next day at 2 pm sharp. When we got there, she was showing us how to make the batter for the *Obst Torte*. A second cake was already baked and cooled. She proceeded to show us how to give it a thin layer of whipped cream, arrange the various berries and fruit in a very appealing way, and top it with glaze. She then presented us with the recipes for both cakes, neatly typed on a manual typewriter. It was just like watching a cooking show. Tante Marie was in her 80th year at that point.

After dad passed away, Tante Marie was able to offer advice to mom based on her experience from losing her husband many years early. Sometimes I would see the two huddle and talk. It was sweet to see the relationship between the two sisters become so close. Tante Marie outlived all her siblings.

Paul Kendler (Onkel Paul)

Onkel Paul was twin to Tante Marie. He was a very handsome man. He married Agnes (Tante Agnes), took over the farm, and raised his family there. Paul was born on Saturday, March 6, 1920.

Tante Agnes learned from mom how to make excellent *Dampfnudel*, a soft airy sweet dumpling that was served with a vanilla sauce. When we visited in 1986, she had gotten mom's huge cast iron *Dampfnudel* pan and treated us to a scrumptious meal. She was awesome in canning fruit and making jams from the bounty of her garden. Tante Agnes had a very sweet personality and was very religious. I loved visiting the farm. Onkel Paul worked the fields; and Tante Agnes would usually tend to the house, cooking, and their three daughters, Pauline, Agi, and Erna. Onkel Paul and mom loved teasing each other. They had a really close relationship.

Onkel Paul's wife died when she was just 69 years old. He had taken her to the village doctor in the morning, the diagnosis was flu. She died that afternoon of a heart attack.

After her death, Onkel Paul frequently came to visit mom to talk things over with her. That always seemed to work out well for them, except one important item. Mom tried to encourage him to write his will. For some reason, he kept putting it off and never got it done. After Onkel Paul died, the youngest daughter Erna claimed that he had told her that he was leaving everything to her. Pauline and Agi wanted the land equally divided as it should be, so their children could get started building their own houses on the property. It finally was settled after an almost 15-year feud. As of 2020 they are on speaking terms, but it's still a little strained.

Tante Agnes and Onkel Paul   ***Onkel Paul***

Pauline, the oldest, was just one year my junior and has been a blessing in our lives. She checks frequently on our family's grave, which is in the old cemetery by the church. Her family has been laid to rest in the new cemetery. Periodically Freda and I send her money to put flowers on our parents' grave on special occasions like birthdays plus Mother's and Father's Day, Christmas, and so on. Pauline always makes sure to order an annual church service to honor mom, dad, and Manfred. As of 2020 this still continues.

Chapter 21

Dad's Family

There is blue blood in the family!

Seeoner Opa and Oma

Dad's parents, Seeoner Oma and Opa, got married on December 26, 1905, and to everyone's best recollection had 21 children. They lived in a very small village of about 10 houses called Wattenham close to castle Seeon, located near Chiemsee.

I can't remember if it was dad's grandfather or great-grandfather who was royalty. Scott remembers my dad talking about this on our visit in 1980. For me, it was Onkel Philipp that shared a little about this in 1982. From what I recall, the grandfather or great-grandfather was royalty and got a chambermaid pregnant. He gave up his royal rights for love and married her. This was considered a Morganatic marriage, which is a marriage between people of unequal social rank. In the context of royalty, this prevents the passage of the husband's titles and privileges to the wife and any children born of the marriage. Generally, this is a marriage between a man of high birth and a woman of lesser status, such as a daughter of a low-ranking noble family or a commoner.

There was a movie made about our family, and my cousin Walter had a small part in it. Onkel Philipp had done a lot of research on this and promised to share everything with me on the next visit in two years. But we always seem to think, next time will come...... and next time never did. Onkel Philipp suffered a heart attack the following year and died.

For some reason, dad never showed much interest in the family history, I am not sure why. Walter died shortly after the movie was made. He had no children, and I was not successful in finding his widow, Gerda, nor was I able to find out more about the movie or the family.

This picture is Oma, Opa, Oma's mother (Frau Haas), Onkel Philipp on the left, dad, and Wally. Ironically these are the three of the 21 children still alive in Oma's last years.

Oma

Dad's mother was Walburga Rauch. To Freda, Manfred, and me, she was Seeoner Oma. She was born on Monday, December 14, 1885, in Uttin near Landsberg and, at the age of 18, married Karl on December 26, 1905.

Their house consisted of a two-bedroom building. Instead of an outhouse, it was an outhouse but inhouse, in the stable behind the goats. There was a water well out back for drinking and washing. Over time, water was brought inside and a second story and a bathroom were added.

By the time I was old enough to have memories of my grandparents, Philipp, my dad, and Wally were the only children left. In reality they had approximately 21 children, and Oma had outlived all but three of her kids. She had lost them to war, malnutrition, tuberculosis, and other illnesses. Three of their daughters, Theresa, Rosa, and Franziska, all died within weeks of each other in 1936 of tuberculosis. They were ages 14, 16, and 17 and worked on a farm. Dad said the farmer had tuberculosis and the girls had to work hard and got very little food. As a matter of fact, what the sick farmer left on his plate was split between the girls. I can only imagine the heartache and agony my grandparents went through. One would never expect to be so poor as not to be able to properly feed one's children and help them out, and most certainly not to outlive them.

I loved my Oma and could not get enough time with her. She gave the most heartfelt hugs and sometimes would hold me so long that I thought she was falling asleep holding me.

Each year Onkel Philipp, Dad, Oma, and I went to church in Seeon on November 2, *Allerseelen* (All Souls Day), which is the day after All Saints Day. On that day we remember all the loved ones we lost. When we put flowers on the family grave, Onkel Philipp and Dad always stood very close to Oma to give her support as she mourned her husband and her children. Those were the only days I ever saw Oma cry. After the service, the four of us went to the *Gasthaus* and had sausages, rolls, beer, or hot tea. Sometimes they would reminisce, and I would be privileged to get a glimpse into old times.

Oma made the best soups but was otherwise not much of a cook. Dad said that Oma could really stretch soups to make sure everyone had something to eat. He jokingly said that, if someone brought a friend home, Oma would count how many kids came through the door and close the door after she got to the number of kids still living at home.

When visiting, Onkel Philipp and Dad would often make repairs and improvements while Oma was showing me off to her neighbors. She liked holding my hand and being close to me, and I had no objections.

Oma was so easy to talk to about things that I did not feel comfortable enough to share with mom or could not find the right time to talk to her about. As a matter of fact, when I met a guy on my 14th birthday and we wanted to write to each other, I had him write the letters to Oma's house. It was our secret. And just before I got married, Oma shared that you do not always have to follow the church's directive to the letter. The example she gave me was that, after many children, she did not want any more and had started practicing the rhythm method for birth control. When she went to confession, the priest told her she had to pray a rosary and give money to God. She replied that she had no problem praying and, if he would give her God's address, she would be sure to mail the money to him.

Oma joined her husband and children in heaven in March 1969 at the age of 83. I was already in America and was not there to give her a last hug. She will always be in my heart.

Opa

Dad's father was Karl Rauch but, to Freda, Manfred, and me, he was Seeoner Opa. He was born on Thursday, January 16, 1879, in Wengen, near Landsberg.

I was only five years old when Opa died. I remember him coming to visit on his bicycle. It was October 15, 1950. He brought us a beautiful porcelain doll. Oma had crocheted a lovely blue dress and hat for her. This was the first doll Freda and I ever had and, because it was the last thing we got from Opa, we were not allowed to play with her.

Opa and mom got along really well. He loved her sense of humor and of course her cooking. Makes sense since Oma mainly made soups. Opa stayed for supper and left in the early afternoon for his eight-mile ride home. When he got there, he sat down on the couch, started taking of his shoes, and began telling Oma how much we loved the doll, what a great visit he had, and what a wonderful meal my mom had put on the table. Those were the last words out of his mouth before he keeled over and died of heatstroke at age 71. Oma and mom never were close before, but it appeared that, after that day, the relationship was even cooler. Maybe Oma thought that if

Opa would not have visited, he would not have died of heatstroke that day. I can only imagine how sad it had to be for all.

Onkel Philipp

Dad's oldest brother was Philipp. He was born on Wednesday, April 29, 1908. He, too, was one of my favorites. He was married to Dora Mueller and had one son, Walter.

Onkel Philipp visited his mother in Seeon frequently as did my dad. Dad usually took me along on the motorcycle, so we got to spend a lot of time together. Onkel Philipp and dad had a close relationship. Onkel Philipp had an injury to his right leg. Whether it was from an accident or the war, I don't know. He was unable to bend his leg, but he still was able to ride the motorcycle. He did not buy a car until after I had moved to America.

Walter was just a couple of years older than me, and we got along very well. He was a big tease, and for some reason I put up with it, silently even enjoying it. He would tell me stories just to see if I caught on to his fibs or not. When I was around 10 years old, Onkel Philipp started to visit us on Good Friday, bring Walter to our house, and take me back to Munich with him for the week. Walter got my mom's wonderful Easter Torte, and I got his chocolates. It was a nice trade-off. Sometimes we would stop for the night in Seeon to visit Oma on the way to Munich, which I was so happy about. I could not get enough of my beloved Oma.

Tante Dora's mother, Frau Mueller, lived with them for all the time I can remember. For many years, Tante Dora and her mom crafted flowers made from very thin foam material. Foam flowers were in. These were the days silk flowers had not been invented yet. There were precut pieces in various colors that needed to be assembled and fastened to wires. This was a job they were commissioned for and a source of income. I loved helping them on my visits. The radio would be playing, or we would just visit and keep our hands busy working on those flowers. Even Onkel Philipp would help. Tante Dora finally stopped this job when her mom passed away.

Cousin Walter married Gerda, a tall and slender woman with a winning personality. They wanted children, but unfortunately it was not in the cards for them. Walter had a small part in a movie made about the Rauch family, and shortly after that he sadly passed away.

After Oma died in 1969, Onkel Philipp and Tante Dora moved from Munich to his remodeled childhood home in Wattenham by Seeon. This put him closer to Chieming and, according to mom, his visits became even more frequent, something both my parents enjoyed. After Tante Dora passed away, he visited at least once a week. I have a sneaking suspicion that Onkel Philipp also wanted a good home-cooked meal, and of course mom would package up a bunch of leftovers for him.

In April 1983, driving home after a visit with my parents, Onkel Philipp suffered a stroke, which caused an accident in which he died. Luckily, no one else was injured. He was only 74 years old.

Mom and Dad, Seeoner Opa, Onkel Philipp and Tante Dora.

My communion, mom, dad, Seeoner Oma,
Freda, Manfred, Walter, and me.

Tante Walburga (Wally)

Tante Wally was born on August 9, 1914, and died March 1, 1969. She was the fifth child. She distanced herself from the family, and I only met her once. I understand she spent most of her life in Trier and was married several times. Her oldest son, Karl, visited us periodically. I believe he wanted family around. Dad was able to provide that for him. Karl was a good-looking young man and worked for the salt mines. His visits continued until 1998 when my dad died. On his last visit Karl shared that, at one time, he had looked up his mother; but she did not recognize him. He gave up after that. How sad!

Chapter 22

My Sister Elfriede, I called her Freda

My sister was born on Monday, May 5, 1941. Mom and dad were very much looking forward to starting a family. With great joy, they welcomed their daughter Elfriede one month before their second wedding anniversary.

Dad carved a beautiful cradle to welcome his first child. As you can see, it was a masterpiece!

*Freda in
the cradle*

Mutti with Freda

Freda was born during World War II. This of course meant that Dad was gone the majority of Freda's early years. He was mostly on the Russian Front and had very few opportunities to come home. It was an uncertain and unsettling time for everyone. The men were gone; and women found themselves fending for themselves and their children. All the while, they worried about the safety of their husbands, fathers, brothers, and sons and wondered if they would ever come home.

Our home was not far from Hitler's hideout, the Eagle's Nest in the Alps. So it was no surprise that American soldiers came to our town. The women were scared and felt vulnerable. When soldiers entered our building, mom was not sure what to expect and was very frightened. Freda remembers that mom made her hide in the closet and told her to be very still and not come out for any reason.

Mom shared some stories with me in later years with the final outcome being that she was able to come to a compromise with the soldier in charge of the troops to take care of his laundry in exchange for some food that was badly needed.

When the war was finally over and dad came home, Freda was a little over four years old. Not having seen her dad often, Freda was confused about why, all of a sudden, this stranger shared a bed with them. She would cry and wanted him to leave. When dad was away at war, mom would always show Freda a picture of dad in uniform and tell her that was her dad. She felt, if dad would put on his uniform and show Freda that he was the same man as in the picture, she would catch on. Dad did this several times until Freda slowly came around.

Freda missed out on a lot of things I was able to do with dad growing up. And her time with mom was also less than perfect because mom had to be the breadwinner while dad was gone. I assume mom was preoccupied at times worrying whether she would ever see dad again. Sadly, these times could not be changed. It was nobody's fault, just circumstances out of their control. Dad, too, missed out on a lot. He did not see his precious little girl stretch her arms out and call him dad, then hug him and sit on his lap. He was not there when she took her first steps. All those "firsts" were missed, and it had to be hard.

Freda was such a beautiful child. There are many photographs of her with mom and dad.

There are very few pictures of me. I don't have a single one with just me and both of my parents. So, if you detect a little jealousy, you are right! I rationalize that our parents were busy trying to build a life after the war and that this was not an easy task.

Freda, me, and a friend of mom's

When I was born, Freda was four and a half years old. As my big sister she was my playmate and my friend. Surely it was fun for her in the beginning, like having your own live doll. However, five years later when our brother Manfred was born, she now fell into a different category of big sister, like teaching me chores around the house and garden, but at the same time watching over our youngest. And of course, she was held responsible for our actions. Over time, fun things became chores and a nuisance. Freda could really get bossy at times. I guess that comes with the territory.

Sometimes we could still find time to have fun together like hula hoops, badminton, or skipping. Freda got rollerskates one time; I don't remember who gave them to her. She was so excited about this gift until she realized it was useless, as most of our roads were gravel.

Freda's closest friend was Emma Klausner, who was one of the daughters of our neighbor, a wellto-do farmer and government representative for Bavaria. One time Freda was at the Klausners' house playing with Emma and Emma's brother, Wolfgang. At one point Freda turned around, and Wolfgang was gone. Quick thinking as she was, Freda realized the sewer lid was left open because the farmer was emptying it to fertilize the fields, and Wolfgang had fallen into the sewer. Quickly she pulled him out in the nick of time. Wolfgang was fine, except he was covered in you-know-what-I-mean and very aromatic.

The time came for Freda to get involved with the traditional dancing group. She was truly the daughter of our parents when it came to that. She was a natural. She had an ear for music, dancing came naturally, and she learned the sometimes complex steps easily and had the looks to go along with it. She had long, thick blond hair that made the most beautiful braids. I remember Freda's dance partner, Kirschbaumer Wastl, sneaking a kiss from her instead of just pretending at the *Fensterl* dance. We teased Freda about that for years. The funny thing was that she did not even like him, but that was her first kiss.

Freda in her traditional outfit.

As Freda got older, she became even prettier. I wanted to be just like her. Unfortunately, my hair was thin and did not lend itself to making nice thick braids like Freda's, I did not feel the beat of the music nor was I a good dancer. I still have not conquered that. I don't think Freda ever realized how much I wanted to be like her.

All the things Freda was required to do – such as helping with building the house, helping with the vacation rental, school, and all things that come along with being the oldest – made her childhood not as sweet as I remember mine. Mom and dad expected us to be as hard-working and committed as they were. Compliments were few as a great job was an expectation. The motto also was work first, play second; however, many times there was no time for play. When we grew up, the words "I love you" were not spoken, you just felt it. That's just the way people were back then.

As I mentioned earlier, Freda was a little bossy, something I believe came from having to take responsibility for her younger siblings as we were growing up. The war had made mom taskoriented and bossy as she juggled jobs and led a hard, hectic life. So mom and Freda collided frequently. Freda had developed a great relationship with Tante Marie, mom's younger sister, and spent a lot of time at the café helping out. The closeness that developed continued until Tante Marie died.

My sister did well in *Volksschule* but had not decided what to do next. She just wanted to be on her own and not be told what to do. So, shortly after Freda's graduation when one of our summer guests who had actually become more like family, Frau Gunst, asked Freda what she was planning to do, her answer was simply to get away from home. Frau Gunst's daughter and her family were on vacation in Chieming as well and, after a short conversation, Freda was hired as apprentice cook. She accepted the job and at age 14 moved to Zweibruecken, 265 miles away from home. Three days later, on September 15, 1955, she was on the bus to begin this new adventure.

Freda worked for Herr and Frau Nierendorf at a restaurant called Jaegerhof in Zweibruecken, Rheinpfalz. She enrolled and completed three years in a trade school specific to her choice of being a chef.

In 1957 Freda was put on as second cook on a probationary basis at the restaurant, She did so well that she was put in charge of the entire kitchen. Her title was "*Selbstaendige Wirtschaftkoechin.*" It is hard to imagine at that young age that she would be in charge of a restaurant kitchen. What an incredible accomplishment!

In May 1958 the restaurant was sold, and Freda went to work for Metzgerei Steinbeck for a few months before moving to Munich, were she took care of Frau Zimmerman.

In September 1958 Freda was out dancing with our Cousin Erna, and the two of them were approached about an opportunity to move to Baumholder. They both accepted.

I had kind of lost contact with Freda after she left in 1955. I had just turned 10 three days earlier, and our brother was not even five years old. So the closeness and continued interaction just was not there. Freda and I reconnected when she came home with an American soldier named Bob. He was a handsome and well-mannered young man. He brought flowers to mom and did everything to show he really wanted to become part of the family.

You could see that Bob and Freda were very much in love. The wedding was planned and the announcement posted at the church. The invitations went out, and I was so excited to get a beautiful new pink brocade dress for the wedding. It was only my third new dress. I normally always had hand-me-downs.

Frau Jackl was almost done with Freda's dress; only the last fitting remained. However, Freda needed to go back to Baumholder to wrap some things up. What happened next, I don't know, except Freda called the wedding off just a few days before the big event. The next time I saw Freda is when she came home to give birth to Carola in April 1961.

I will never forget Carola's birth. It was a difficult one for sure as the baby was breech. Frau Falkinger, our much-liked town midwife who had delivered Freda, Manfred, and me, had suffered a heart attack; so a midwife that we did not know came to the house. Freda went into labor on Saturday morning and gave birth Monday night, April 24. I remember the screams and was terrified of getting pregnant. Emma, Freda's best friend, came by and sat with her periodically. Emma became Carola's Godmother. Freda and Emma stayed close until Emma passed away.

Carola stayed with us while Freda continued to work in northern Germany. Mom, dad, myself, and Manfred were able to spend the first couple of years with Carola. Manfred and dad of course had the most opportunity to be with her. Manfred became especially attached to Carola and dragged her all over the place.

Freda and Carola

In the fall of 1961 Freda came to visit and brought Pat with her. Pat was there to ask my parents for Freda's hand in marriage. Steve was Pat's best friend and came along for moral support.

Steve and I fell in love and, on January 16, 1963, we had a double civil ceremony in Baumholder. Just the four of us plus Agi and Roy, friends of Pat and Steve, as our witnesses. The guys were due to be shipped out, and there was no time to plan a wedding or wait for our parents to join us. I am sure that too, had to be tough on mom and dad.

Chapter 23

Do You Remember?

It was so great to reminisce with Freda about some of the fun, sad, quirky, or just everyday occurrences from our childhood. So here is a collection of some of what we came up with.

Clean Plate Club

Our house was a clean plate club. If you did not finish what was on your plate, you got it at the next meal and the next meal until it was gone. The motivation was that we did not have a refrigerator. Need I say more? It did not happen very often, but sometimes it was just something we did not like. I have to say, we never went hungry. Even if it was a pot of rice made on Monday and we had it with gravy one day, applesauce the next, etc.

There was only one exception to the clean plate club per person. Freda did not have to eat raw onions, and I did not have to eat creamed spinach. I don't remember what our brother did not have to eat. I think he ate everything. He, too, inherited moms cooking talents and put it to use many years later in his *Wirtschaft* in the Alps.

Acorn Collecting

Freda and I liked making extra money. We knew where the best acorn trees were, so every year we collected acorns and farmers paid us 5 DM per sack. Farmers used acorns for pig food.

Peat for Warmth in the Winter

Seeoner Oma had a place she could get peat. Every year Freda and I would go with mom and dad to get peat for Seeoner Oma to keep her warm in the wintertime. Peat is something that forms in wetlands with a high acid content. The acidity prevents the marshy plants, including trees, grasses, and moss, from fully decaying. This partly decayed organic material builds up and over millions of years becomes peat. Peat is thick, muddy, and looks like dark bricks.

Mom and dad used edging shovels to cut out rectangles. We helped load it and, once we got it home, it would be dried and stacked just like wood. We had to be very careful of *Kreuzottern* which favored this moist area. Back in the 50s, *Kreuzottern* were Germany's only deadly snakes. I am still deathly afraid of snakes.

Potato Harvest

Frequently during harvest time, we had to help the farmers in the field. Mom and Freda got paid 5 Marks a day (about $1.25 at the time) and lunch. Because of my age, I worked just for the food.

One time we worked the potatoes for Klausner. They would plow the potatoes up with a tractor, and we would gather them. We were going along filling the baskets when, suddenly, my mom started screaming and pulled off her sweatpants. Freda and I thought she had lost it and, of course, felt very embarrassed seeing mom strip down to her underwear. Well, we finally saw what had happened. Mom had stepped into a mouse nest, and all these baby mice were running up her legs. Once we knew what had happened, it was actually pretty hilarious.

At the end of the potato harvest day, we turned the crates over and sat down to rest. We were tired but felt good knowing we did a good job and had a great harvest. The dried vegetation was now being burned, and we each got to roast a potato. It was a treat and they tasted awesome. In retrospect, I don't know if it was because we were hungry or if they really were that good.

Learning to Lace Crochet

At one time we rented two rooms to Frau Streit. Her grandson was the local stone mason who in later years would actually make my parents' gravestone. Frau Streit was alone a lot, and sometimes I would visit her and keep her company. I remember her teaching me to crochet lace around handkerchiefs. I made many and enjoyed giving them as gifts. I wish I had kept one. Frau Streit was with us for two years before she passed.

Church Clock, or Page Me!

We did not have wristwatches growing up. We would rely on the church clock to know when to head home. If we were at a friend's house and did not pay attention, or mom needed us to come home early, she just cupped her hands on the mouth and called our name. The next person who heard it passed it on. There was no mistaking in a small village like ours when you were being paged.

Butterleaf Lettuce

Dad loved the firm and crispy center of the butterleaf lettuce we grew in our garden. When this salad was served, he always tried to find the center. Just in case you tried to make a move for it, you got slapped on the hand with his fork. It became a game with us. Of course, we always let him have his way, and he knew it.

Chocolate Treats

In the wintertime mom would let us make chocolates. She had these cute little molds in various patterns; they were about 1 ½ inches big. She would fill a large bowl with fresh fallen snow. Then she would make the chocolate while we arranged the molds in the snow and carefully pushed them down to the rim so the cold snow would set the chocolate.

We sat around the kitchen table and filled the molds with the melted chocolate, and then the wait began. Well, sometimes by accident or on purpose, we drizzled a little on the snow, which of course set up right away; and we got a taste of what was to come later. Those were some things she did for Freda, Manfred and me to show her love.

Dad's Cigarettes

Dad made a cutting board with an attached knife for mom to cut the bread for dumplings. He made a miniature version for himself to cut tobacco leaves. After the war, everyone could grow a certain number of plants. So dad grew his own tobacco, hung it on the clothesline on the balcony to dry, cut it, and then rolled his own cigarettes. He smoked his cigarettes down as far as possible. It was really funny to see the tobacco leaves hanging on the clothesline.

Trick or Treat

We were never allowed to go. Dad felt it was a way of begging. He was a very proud man. However, we were allowed to dress up and participate in the *Fasching* parade and party Onkel Hans put together every year when he was alive. Mom was great at making costumes or helping us put one together. She knew how much fun we always had at *Fasching*.

In this picture with my sister and Erna (the daughter of mom's cousin Fanny), I still have scabs on my face from crashing my sled, face first, into the hut at the bottom of the hill. Reinhard, our doctor's son, who I went to school with, talked me into lying face down on the sled, and he sat on my back pretending I was his horse and down the hill we went. It did not end well!

Playing Games

When we first moved into our house, we had a lot more free time because dad would be home in the evenings and on weekends; and mom did not have to work for the Baroness anymore. All that was left was getting the garden set up and placing odds and ends around to make everything look pretty.

Those were the family times I will always treasure. Music, laughter, and playing games like *Federball* (badminton). Freda and I had hula hoops that were another source of fun and exercise. I never got the hang of card games; it seemed to me that the rules changed periodically so mom could win. Our cousins, my sister, and I still joke about it.

Letter from Mom – her sense of humor was incredible

After dad had passed and mom had been in the hospital again around the time of his death, once she got home, our brother tried to convince Freda and me that mom was getting extremely forgetful. We did not feel that way when we talked with her every week. So imagine our surprise when Freda and I each got a handwritten letter from mom. Translated into English, it said:

Dear Son,

The next time you come home you will not recognize the place. We moved! The new house came with a washing machine. I put a shirt in it, pulled the chain, and have not seen it since. Your uncle Philipp drowned in a whiskey barrel; since he wanted to be cremated, the flames did not go out for three days. Your sister is pregnant, I don't know if you are going to be an aunt or uncle as we don't know if she is having a girl or a boy. We had such a bad earthquake last week that the chicken laid the same egg three times. I wanted to send you some money but had already sealed the envelope.

Love, Mom

Now Freda and I were worried. We called mom and asked how she was doing, and she started laughing and asked if we got her letter. She said, "I heard this joke and had to write it out for you."

Socks

When mom sent packages, she always made sure Freda and I got the same things. She did not play favorites. So here is a funny story.

One time I received my package with coffee, chocolate, and three socks, not two pair, but three socks. I called Freda and shared that maybe our brother was right, perhaps mom was getting forgetful.

Freda did not say much, but a few days later I received an envelope from her with a sock and a note that said: being the older and wiser, I knew exactly what to do with my extra sock. I did tell mom about it. She laughed and figured she must have taken the socks out of the wrong box. She always matched up socks and tied them together at the toe with a piece of yarn. We had a good laugh.

Chapter 24

My Brother Manfred

in later years he insisted on being called Fred.

His friends nicknamed him Schufti.

My brother was born on Friday, March 9, 1951, the only grandson to Egerer Oma and Opa. All of mom's siblings had girls.

Just like me, there are not a lot of pictures taken when Manfred was little. Those were busy days as my parents were occupied working and building the house at the same time. As you can see from the picture on his first day in school, my brother was a good-looking kid.

Manfred 1ˢᵗ day in school

After Freda left, Manfred and I continued the tradition of joining Onkel Hans for the *Fasching* Parade. My brother loved cowboy stories, so no wonder he dressed up as cowboy and talked me into being a dance hall girl. We did have fun when I had time and he was in the mood. Manfred had a cute smile and I distinctly remember how he giggled when he felt he had pulled one over on you. No question about it, he was cute.

I remember him as also being very curious. One day I found Manfred lying on the cement next to the house looking down the small basement window to my summer room. My cat, Muschi, was down there on a little bed I made her as it was her time to be a mommy for the first time and I did not want anyone to bother her. I asked Manfred what he was doing, and his answer was, "I have to know." Of course, I asked for further clarification, and he said he wanted to know how the kittens come out of her tummy, does she spit them or sh.. them? Mom and I could not stop laughing.

Manfred was barely eight when dad had that horrible accident. Those were the years dad would have taken my brother on nature walks, mushroom picking and all the wonderful things I had enjoyed at his age. Sadly, that was not going to happen. There seemed not to be a lot of time for Manfred: dad was not home for 1 ½ years, mom was working like crazy to make ends meet, Freda was in the north pursuing her career, and I was going to Sparz and working.

It was a blessing in disguise when Carola was born and stayed with us. Manfred looked at her as his charge and did everything to make her happy. He was a happy camper.

Manfred and Carola

After Freda, Carola, and I left for the States, Mom spoiled him rotten, which is easy to understand because he was the only child left at home. Manfred got together again with the only bad boys in the village that he had hooked up with before Carola was born. He got into all kinds of trouble, sold some of my parents belongings like a fabulous album cover dad had carved, but also got physically hurt messing around one day and ended up in the hospital with his leg in traction.

I don't know all the details, but one of the boys was angry with him, went to the hospital, kicked the leg that was in traction, and caused irreversible damage. Manfred ended up with a permanent limp that stopped him from enjoying many activities a boy his age would want to participate in. His bad-boy syndrome continued after he recovered, and he ended up in jail during his teen years. While in jail, he saved a young man's life. The young man was released about the same time as Manfred and made it his goal to straighten my brother out. And he succeeded.

In later years Manfred opened a *Gasthaus* in Siegsdorf and became known as someone you could count on. He was married and had two boys, Holger and Alexander, by his first wife, Elfriede. Manfred and his second wife, Ingrid, had a very successful business and expanded the *Gasthaus* by adding a play area for children. It was at the *Gasthaus* that Manfred reconnected with his illegitimate son, Alexander, whom he had not seen since birth. Alex and his wife, Sandy, moved into an apartment in Manfred's house and worked with him until he died at age 56 of asthma. Manfred had the pleasure of enjoying a grandchild by Alex and Sandy. Tamara was the apple of his eye, and Nico was born shortly after Manfred's death.

The *Gasthaus* had a great reputation. The traditional dancers had their meetings there. Manfred orchestrated many fun activities and, after his death, his widow was able to sell the restaurant and the three-story building with four apartments for top dollar. She was able to retire at age 55 and moved to the wine country to join her family.

After my brother's funeral, we heard about all the wonderful things Manfred had done to raise money for orphans, among other good deeds. The emails and letters we received were heartwarming as was the knowledge that he had turned his life around and had become a respected and beloved member of the community.

I love this picture of my brother, mom, and
dad. Dad has that look of love!

Chapter 25

My Parents

Mom and dad waited eight long years to get a blessing to marry from mom's parents. Family was important, so mom and dad made the sacrifice and waited until 1939 to wed. They both loved music, dancing, the outdoors, our beautiful Alps, and our lake. They shared the dream of wanting to build their own home and raise their family there.

But World War II interrupted their dreams.

Once the war was over in 1945, mom and dad reaffirmed their commitment to build their own home. Ingenuity, commitment, experience, and five years of hard work and sacrifices made that dream come true in 1954.

Once more, their dreams and hopes were shattered when dad had a devastating accident in 1959 which affected the rest of their lives in a major way.

These circumstances forced Mom to take on the stronger, traditionally more masculine role in the family. She had to do all the heavy lifting, making sure enough money was coming in to pay the bills and to put food on the table. She had to be the disciplinarian and teacher of life's everyday lessons. Mom and dad balanced each other out so well, and dad transitioned to the nurturer role almost seamlessly. I am sure it was not as easy for mom and dad as it seemed to me. They did what needed to be done without question and without complaint.

1963 brought yet another challenge. Freda, I, and their first grandchild, Carola, all left within a few months for America, which left them alone with my 12-year-old brother. I am sure their hearts were breaking!

Their bond was strong! Dad died on October 30, 1998, and over the next seven years mom would get sick and end up in the hospital around the time of dad's death. In 2005 she was in the hospital again, and this time it seemed more serious. On November 30, 2005, my brother was able to let me talk to mom on the phone. When we hung up, she asked my brother what the date was and when he told her it is the 30th, she said,*"Dann ist es ja gut"* (then that's good) and closed her eyes to join dad in heaven.

In the next two chapters I would like to share with you what my parents were all about, what they enjoyed, how they dealt with difficult times and accepted challenges, how they related to each other and supported each other, and how they complemented each other to make their marriage work for 59 ½ years.

Chapter 26

Dad – I Called Him Papa

My dad, Anton Rauch was the third of 21 children and was born Saturday, July 9, 1910 in Maisach/ Fuerstenfeldbruck. He was raised in Wattenham near Seeon.

In dad's family there were always more mouths to feed than there was food. So, at age 11, my dad was sent to a farmer who needed him for work. In exchange the farmer would take care of dad's needs and make sure he got to go to Sunday school. Sunday school was something created to help children to continue to learn to read and write, etc., as many families found themselves in situations like dad's family.

The farmer had several horses, and dad loved caring for them. The farmer treated my dad very much like his own son. It was during that time that dad started playing around with wood carving. Dad worked for the farmer until he married mom and moved to Pfaffing.

The War

Dad was drafted into the German Army and was made a medic even though he had no medical experience. He manned a horse-drawn ambulance. Dad was in France for a short while and, after that, spent most of the time in Russia. He felt that soldiers who did not agree with Hitler's philosophy were sent to the most dangerous war front where they were more likely to draw fire. Dad felt this was the reason he was sent to the Russian front.

Many years later I asked my dad about a particular picture of him standing in a field of tall grass. I was always drawn to that picture and wanted to know more about it. Dad shared that, on that day, he received a commendation for saving lives. A number of wounded soldiers needed to be brought to safety. The only way to get them out was across an ice-cold river where the water was chest deep. Dad and the other soldiers had to carry the wounded over their heads to save them. He said they were able to bring every one of them across the river. However, several of the soldiers carrying the wounded through the freezing river in Russia perished.

I remember my dad generally did not want to talk about the war. But on that day, he finally shared a little with me. He talked about how freezing cold Russia was, how they lacked warm clothes and other supplies they needed, and how frequently they were starving.

My dad was shot and badly wounded in Russia. I don't recall the details except that Russian farmers found him. They cared for his wounds, hid him from the Russian soldiers, and nursed him back to health. Dad always wanted to go back to thank them for saving his life but, even after the war, that would have posed a danger to the very people he wanted to thank.

At some point, dad reunited with his unit, but how and where I don't know. Dad was captured twice and escaped the first time. The second time was in Rimini, Italy. In captivity his jailors realized dad knew how to care for horses and used him for that purpose. During that time dad using a twig and tail hair from the horses crafted a long chain to pass the time. He brought that chain home with him.

A couple of times over the years, mom and I would sit and talk about when dad was away at war. She shared how she often wondered if he was cold or hungry, and she worried if he was wounded or worse.

Mom told me how fiercely she prayed for dad's safe return! She talked about the few times he was able to come home and how bittersweet those times were, because they both knew dad had to leave again with no certainty of seeing each other once more.

Mom explained how she had to change and become a stronger and more self-sufficient woman. She had to be mom and dad, provider and protector for my sister Freda, who was 4 ½ years old when dad finally came home in 1945. Mom said that she would take dad's photograph down from the dresser each day, show it to Freda, and tell her, "That's your dad and he will try to come home soon." All the time, mom said she had a lump in her throat and silently worried about dad's safety.

Homecoming

Finally, the war was over and dad came home. Most certainly he had changed after the horrors of war. He also found his wife had changed – she had gone through tough times as well and was now used to making her own decisions. His daughter did not recognize him anymore and wanted this stranger to go away. Many times, dad would change back into his uniform and stand next to the picture mom had shown Freda every day until she finally realized that he really was her dad.

And then there came a new baby, me! Dad was there for my birth plus all the firsts: the first smile, giggle, hug, word, and step. We formed a strong bond from that day on. I was the lucky one!

Dad buried a gun in the back yard. He said he never wanted to be without protection again. At the beginning of Hitler's regime, gun registration became mandatory. Later, if you had not joined the Nazi party or if you did not openly agree with Hitler's philosophy, your guns were collected. I am sure that is the reason why I am so against gun control.

The Priceless Chandelier

While looking for work, Dad took up carving again. He liked using pine as it was the best wood for carving. Dad always said it was like carving butter. Dad, mom, and Freda all needed shoes; and money was tight. Dad was very resourceful and shared with mom his idea of carving a special chandelier for the shoemaker in exchange for three pairs of shoes.

Dad designed a chandelier consisting of six panels. He carved each panel with the image of a forest animal. There was a deer with a doe, a squirrel, a rabbit, an Ibex (mountain goat), a fox, and a pheasant. Dad hung the chandelier with the chain he had made from horsehair while in captivity. Mom finished the chandelier off by lining the lampshade with a beautiful green silk. Leiterman, the local shoemaker, was stunned by the craftsmanship and could not say yes fast enough to the proposed trade. Below is picture of the chandelier proudly displayed in the shoemaker's living room.

Freda and I were unsuccessful in attempting to buy it back. We tried on almost every visit back to Germany to accomplish that, to no avail. Rudl, the shoemaker's eldest son, told me on my last visit that he might consider it sometime in the future. I tried again in 2018 and sent a letter to Rudl. I received a reply from Bernhard, Rudl's son and the shoemaker's grandson. He explained that, after the death of his grandfather, the younger son Michael was given the house with everything in it including the chandelier. Michael died shortly thereafter, and the house was sold. His widow does not remember what happened to the chandelier. So regretfully they were unable to help me. There is nothing I can do except treasure the memory.

Dad's Jobs

Dad found work with the local furniture maker, Ellmaier. Both knew that dad would not be working many hours because not a lot of people could afford new furniture. However, it was a start and a great learning experience for dad.

Finally, dad secured a position with Thiele, a builder in Traunstein. He started out operating the tall crane. His job sometimes took him out of town for a week at a time because Thiele built houses throughout Germany. Dad knew he did not have to worry about anything at home as he could always count on mom.

On one job in Munich, dad operated a huge crane. One day a bad storm was approaching, and the light on the tip of the crane arm did not light up. Dad had to climb out on the crane arm to fix the light

GROWING UP IN BAVARIA

or attach a lantern, and he fell. He must have had a special angel looking out for him that day, because someone had left a manhole cover off at the construction site below and dad fell right into the sewer. The only thing broken was his watch that he hit on the side of the manhole.

Dad Liked his Beer

Dad preferred dark beer and, in the winter, he used a beer warmer. In the summer dad wanted it cold. Sometimes he would drink wheat beer. At home with *Brotzeit* (an afternoon snack) or with his meals, he drank *Radler*, beer mixed with clear lemonade like 7-Up. Dad sometimes got stuck at Oberwirt or Tante Marie's café on Sunday mornings after church. Yet he wanted his pork roast and dumplings ready at 11:30 am when he got home.

If mom realized dad would be late for supper and the dumplings would get soggy, she would send me to get him. A phone call was not an option as we did not have a phone. Besides, dad responded pretty well to my coaxing him to coming home.

Dad also liked his beer on Saturday night with all the other men in town. At times, though, he could get carried away, get drunk, come home late, and spend more money than he should have. Mom did not like it when dad drank too much. Those are the times they would argue and yell, and sometimes break a dish or two. Then they would give each other the silent treatment for a couple of days. And suddenly, like sunshine after rain, everything was fine again.

Dad's Fun Activities

Dad was involved in many community activities and clubs. Some had to do with music, nature, and trails. One of the activities I know he enjoyed immensely was being an actor in the local theater. The performances were held at Unterwirt. The cast always got together early, had dinner and, of course, beer. At one performance, I remember dad had come home from a job and had not slept yet. He changed clothes and met the cast for dinner and beer. Did I mention that dad liked his beer?

And on that day, being tired, the beer must have hit dad harder. That was apparent when the show started. In the script, dad was to have a rip on the seat of his pants fixed while dressed, and he was to react when he accidentally got stuck by the needle. Well, he nodded off, the actress actually stuck him with the needle, he yelled "ouch!", and the act was right on track again. In the picture below, dad is the tallest man on the left. He played the bum in that performance. The Pletschacher Brothers, Max and Bernhard, were dad's best friends. In this picture, Max is in the cue box, and Bernhard is smoking the pipe.

A Dream Cut Short

Dad always wanted to provide for all of us the very best he could. I also think he was always trying to prove that he could provide for my mom better than Andreas, the postal worker my grandparents had wanted my mom to marry.

So, when dad's employer, Thiele, had secured a one-year job in Australia and chose dad as a crew member, mom and dad made the decision that being apart for one year would be a sacrifice they were willing to make to ensure a secure financial future. Dad was going to leave at the end of May or the beginning of June in 1959. However, that was not in the cards for them. The details of the horrible accident on Friday, May 1, that I described in the chapter "a life-changing event" ended up with dad's being away from home for about one and a half years. When dad finally came home, it was on crutches because the prostheses did not work for him. Money was tight, and mom continued to struggle to make ends meet.

Wood Carving

Dad was trying to figure out how to help financially and what to do with the rest of his life. Opportunities are few in small towns like Chieming and the surrounding areas. So as time went by, dad went back to wood carving. He became such an expert at it that people who needed an antique repaired anywhere in Germany or parts of Austria would come seek him out. He could have made a lot of money carving and selling things, but dad was not money-hungry; he was a perfectionist and wanted to provide something special that made people happy.

If someone dad liked and respected asked him to carve a cradle or hope chest, he would do it and just charge the bare minimum. If it was someone dad did not feel good about, they could not have paid him enough to entice him. He carved cradles, jewelry boxes, serving trays, umbrella holders, sewing boxes, picture frames, hope chests, coffee tables and end tables, and even the pillars at the local restaurant.

My son Scott has the very first two picture frames dad carved at age 11. Dad had such a talent and passion for carving that it became his lifelong calling. Dad's four grandchildren here in the USA each have a cradle he carved and various other pieces. In the entrance of my home is a shadow box that contains a tabletop my dad carved while visiting us in Santa Barbara. Scott and dad went for a walk one day and came back with some beautiful leaves. Dad started carving that tabletop while visiting and incorporated that leaf in the pattern. What a treasure!

Dad's Love for the Outdoors

Dad loved the outdoors, nature, horses, birds, and all kinds of critters. Our village and surrounding communities formed a walking club. The route and its length were predetermined, and frequently some of the trails were through beautiful, wooded areas. Medals were presented to each walker that finished the route. Dad joined the club and received many medals and awards. There were no accommodations made for the handicapped; dad walked the same route as all other members with the exception that he walked on crutches. My son Scott went on one of those adventures with my dad on our visit in 1980. Scott shares the same fondness for nature as my dad.

Some of Dad's medals

Dad and Me

I enjoy thinking back to the evenings dad and I listened to radio programs. Sometimes we would have different interpretations and views. Dad always encouraged me to form my own opinions but also cautioned me that this was a two-way street and to respect the opinions of others.

As I look back I realize, because dad's dream was cut short, this enabled me to spend precious time with him. I am so grateful for everything he taught me over the years. Dad was an honest, proud, and caring man. He had a hard life but never complained. He did his best to make a good and meaningful life for his family. He was a good son, great brother, caring and supportive husband, and an incredible father.

I loved my dad with all my heart and will always treasure the many wonderful memories of our times together.

Chater 27

Mom – I Called Her Mutti

My mom, Therese Kendler, was born on Saturday, September 6, 1913, in Paulfisch/Siegsdorf. She was the eldest of five children of Therese and Johann Kendler. She grew up on a farm in Egerer, about eight miles from Seeon, where dad grew up.

From an early age on, mom was expected to work on the farm just like all other family members. She was also expected to be an example for her younger siblings and teach them the ropes. The following picture of Eggerer Oma, mom, and two of her siblings was taken in 1919. You may notice in the picture that mom's shoes look very big. Because she was the eldest, shoes were bought for her and later passed down to younger siblings. Her shoes were bought several sizes too big and had to be worn with several pairs of socks. As her feet grew, she wore less socks. Having the shoemaker resole the shoes was less expensive than new shoes.

A couple of times over the years, mom and I would talk about when dad was away at war. She shared how she often wondered if he was cold or hungry, and how she worried about his safety. She talked about the few times he was able to come home, how they treasured their time together, and how gut wrenching it was to part, because there was no certainty that they would see each other again.

Mom explained how she had to change and become a stronger and more self-sufficient woman. She tried to be mom and dad for my sister Freda. She said that, when dad was gone, she would take dad's photograph down from the dresser every day, show it to Freda, and tell her, "That's your dad and he will try to come home soon." All the time she said she had a lump in her throat and silently worried about dad's safety.

My parents shared a love for cats and always had several. All of us kids must have inherited that because we love cats as well. Peterl was dad's cat, trained to jump clear across the kitchen table when dad gave him the signal. All cats were trained not to attack birds. Dad loved watching the birds from the patio and would get really upset if a stray cat attempted to catch one. Dad loved all critters. He was so happy when white horses were corralled on the property adjacent to our house.

Below is a picture of mom and me with my favorite cat, Muschi. This picture was taken just a few months before I got married.

Mom, Muschi and me

Mom the Cook

Mom was known to be an excellent cook. Chieming had two restaurants. One was in the lower village by the lake, appropriately called Unterwirt; the other was on the upper side and called Oberwirt. Weddings in our village always included most everyone in town as everyone knew each other. It was a good money maker for the restaurant. Everyone had to pay for their own meal. The bride and groom were only responsible for the meals and drinks their parents, grandparents, and godparents consumed.

When a wedding was planned at Oberwirt, the owners would always check mom's availability to help cook before they committed to a date. Everyone in town knew my mom's cooking and would rave about it. Frequently she was asked for recipes; however, she only had written recipes for cakes and cookies.

When we were growing up, we only had a wood burning stove in the kitchen that had four burners on top, an oven, and a water tank that kept the water hot for doing dishes. Mom did all her cooking and baking on that stove. How she knew how many pieces of wood to put in the fire to get the right temperature for cookies and cakes and roasts, I will never know. I don't think anyone can top her pork roast with bread dumplings and gravy. Or her potato and cucumber salad. Mom made the two salads separately and then mixed them together.

Cucumber salad is easy; the dressing was vinegar, oil, salt, and a pinch of sugar. The potato salad is not so easy to imitate. The potatoes mom used were very much like the Yukon gold potatoes in America, light, buttery-tasting, and a little on the sweet side. I remember mom used melted butter instead of oil on the potatoes, but I don't remember anything else. Freda and I have tried many times to copy that salad but have not been successful.

When elderberries were in bloom, mom would get them from our neighbor, batter dip the flowers, deep fry them, and then dust them with powdered sugar. What a scrumptious dessert! We looked forward to elderberry blooming time each year.

Elderberry Flower Dessert Recipe

Wash and dry the flowers.
Make a thin pancake batter using the following ingredients:
1 3/4 cups flour
2 eggs
1/2 cup milk
1/2 tsp. salt
1/2 tsp. cinnamon, optional12-16 elderberry blossoms
with stems
oil for frying

Heat oil in a high-sided frying pan – oil should be about ½ inch high.

Dip the dry flowers in the batter, shake off excess batter, and fry for about two minutes until golden brown.

Serve warm dusted with powdered sugar and enjoy!

Mom made the best cakes and cookies. Christmas cookies were awesome, and there is more about that in the Christmas story. Easter was another special baking time. Mom went all out and made a sinful cake with lots of eggs and layers of butter cream. The cake was decorated with little chocolate nests with a couple of sugary eggs in them. We usually did not have butter, because that came from Egerer Opa and Oma's farm and they sold the butter for money. But we always had butter for the Easter cake. What a treat!

Mom the Organizer

Mom was a stickler for cleanliness and organization. Our house was always perfectly clean and organized, and her expectations were high. Everything that was washed, except for towels, had to be ironed. When mom took on more and more laundry jobs, she bought a "mangel" which is an ironing machine that you could use for flat items like sheets, handkerchiefs, T-shirts, and so on.

We did not have built-in closets in Bavaria, we had standalone wardrobe closets with hang-up room on one side and shelves on the other. Mom would periodically inspect how organized we kept our rooms. If the folded clothes were sloppy and not lined up properly, she pulled everything out; and we had to rewash everything, which was a three-step process as we did not have a washing machine and dryer. Clothes were washed in various tubs depending on the temperature needed, rinsed in other tubs, and then hung on the line to dry. Of course, ironing and folding was the next step. It definitely was over the top but taught us a lesson.

I think that stuck with me. I try to be very neat and organized. Sadly, with mom's glaucoma, in her late 80s, she could no longer see well; and her attention to detail suffered.

Mom's Likes and Dislikes

Mom did not like roses because they had thorns, and she was allergic to primroses which made her break out in hives. But she loved peonies and had planted light pink and dark pink varieties in her garden all along the street side. They were a sight to be seen. We were able to pick enough in June 1989 for their 50th wedding anniversary to decorate all the tables at Oberwirt for the dinner celebration.

Mom was a stickler on manners. I think "please" and "thank you" were taught before the word candy was spoken. It took a lot to make mom mad but, if you did, watch out: she dished out a punishment you would not easily forget. I remember her periodic reminders at the dinner table, "Get your elbows off the table!"

Mom did not like people that took advantage of others, and she did not easily forget if you did something that hurt her deeply. And sometimes she would forget to filter what she said.

Mom's Closest Friends: Luise, Resl, and Anni

Resl and mom were friends since 1939, when my parents moved to Pfaffing. Mom was godmother to six of her seven children and took that honor very seriously. I shared more about that in the story about the Dangl family.

Luise, the wife of dad's friend Max, was one of mom's best friends for over 40 years. They had a farm down the hill which had the pond I almost drowned in (that, too, is covered in another story). Luise and mom loved baking together, playing cards, and going to the traditional dance and theater performances. Unfortunately they had a falling out when they were both in their 80s. One time when they were talking, mom shared with Luise that, when my brother was a young kid, he did something really stupid and ended up in jail. The story got out and, because my brother now owned and operated a restaurant, it did not go over well. Mom was hurt that Luise betrayed the confidence; the hurt never healed, and regretfully the relationship was never repaired.

The friendship with Anni began in 1954, shortly after our house was finished, Dad's boss Oswald and his wife Anni were building a house up the street from us. During construction, Oswald got laid off. Things were tight financially. Mom suggested to Anni that she be her partner on some cleaning jobs so that Anni could supplement her income. Mom also helped them out with food, veggies from the garden, and whatever else we could spare.

Anni never forgot the help she got from mom. They remained very close friends and confidants – so much so that, after my mom passed in 2005, Anni would ride to the graveyard on her bicycle to water the plants and make sure a candle was burning. In Bavaria, the graves are often covered with live plants and flowers. Last time I visited my parents' grave in 2010, I saw a bicycle leaning against the cemetery wall and I knew right away it was Anni. Even though Anni was in her late 80s at the time, she was watering and making sure there were no weeds. Anni and I hugged and cried and, when I asked her why she continued doing this, her reply was that she could never repay my mom for all she did for her when they were in need.

Anni continued this special labor of love until her daughter moved her to a retirement home in Munich in 2015.

How Mom Showed Love

During the times we grew up, the words "I love you" were not often spoken. However, you felt it. For instance, because Mom lived through very hard times, she was an avid saver and worked hard for every penny she had. On visits, when she gave us children money, she was really saying, "I love you!"

When we visited in later years, mom remembered what sweets or foods we liked and made sure she had them ready for us. There was always chocolate in our bedroom. She called it *Bett Hupferl* (something to jump in bed with). She loved taking us to visit her friends and showing us off when we visited. My voice sounds a lot like my mom and, frequently when we were at home and I answered mom's phone, the caller would say *"Gruess Dich, Resi,"* thinking I was her. I also look a lot like my mom, I even have her hips. Ha, ha! The only thing I did not get was mom's beautiful hair, Freda was lucky enough to get that. Somehow, I ended up with dad's hair genes.

Mom sent Freda and me our favorite German coffee. The packages came like clockwork. For over 20 years, I never had to buy coffee in the US. Mom always included chocolate, *Lebkuchen*, or socks. It was really a tearful day when her last package arrived after she had already gone to heaven. I know she is looking down at us.

My Mom!

After dad's accident in 1959, when suddenly we had to do without his income, it was crystal clear just what an incredible strong woman mom was. She added more and more jobs to make ends meet. She was responsible for everything during the one and a half years dad was in the hospital. She did laundry and ironing for people, cleaned newly built houses before move-in, delivered telegrams, cleaned the post office, worked with farmers in the field, chopped wood, helped her sister Marie at the café, tended to the garden, and still took care of us and our home. She also made sure everything was perfect for the rooms we rented out in the summer. I never heard mom complain.

During that tough time, I was still going to college and had several jobs to make sure I had enough money for tuition, so I was not able to help mom a lot. It still amazes me when I think about all the things mom had to do and manage during that time. She easily could have made me drop out of college and help bring in money, but that was never even brought up. On top of that, for the last three months of college, I was unable to come up with all the tuition money. With no questions asked, mom made up the difference. She was an incredibly strong woman and had a heart of gold. My sister was not home during those tough times, and I wish she would have been there to see that side of mom.

Mom's transportation finally improved from a bicycle to a moped. That was still tough in the rain and in the wintertime, but better than before; and she always managed. Sunday was *"Ruhetag,"* the day of rest. We went to church; feasted on our traditional pork roast, dumplings, and gravy; and enjoyed the rest of the day whenever we were not scheduled to work.

Mom loved strong coffee; it was a ritual to make it. She used a manual grinder for her coffee beans, placed the grounds in the paper filter, and then poured boiling water over the grounds ever so slowly. To see her on a Sunday afternoon listening to her favorite music station, enjoying her coffee and a piece of plum cake (called *Zwetschgendatschi*) or *Nusstorte* (hazelnut layer cake), you would think mom was in heaven. She was perfectly happy spending the afternoon sitting there, knitting and sometimes nodding. I think at one point everyone in our village had mittens, caps, or socks that she had made for them. Everyone knew mom and, on her birthday, we would sometimes need two tables to hold all her cards, flowers and gifts.

Dad was disabled for 40 years, and for the last 15 years he was confined to a wheelchair with Mom nursing him. Mom suffered from glaucoma and battled advanced arthritis. Her knees were bone on bone, and injections would make it better for only a few days. However, mom would continue getting the shots when she could. She said it was worth having a few days with less pain.

Taking care of dad was hard on mom, and I remember sitting in the kitchen with her just talking after dad died. She shared that, even though sometimes harsh words were spoken, she missed him very much. She also admitted that she felt relieved not having to care for him day and night, and that made her feel guilty. We hugged and cried. I think I was finally able to get mom to understand that it was normal to feel relief after caring for dad for so long and having a hard time herself. That does not mean she loved him less. At the time of my dad's passing, they had been married for 59 ½ years.

Mom lived to the age of 92 and spent the last six months at my brother's place in Siegsdorf, about 15 miles from where she had spent most of her life. She could no longer walk the stairs and was isolated up on the second floor. Her physical needs were taken care of. But I know she was very lonely. However, she never complained. Her sister and some of her nieces and godchildren who lived in the area would periodically visit.

After mom passed, her closest friend, Anni, shared with me that my sister-in-law, Ingrid, had mom declared incompetent even though mom was sharp as a tack. Ingrid had connections and obviously wanted to control mom's assets. I was 6,000 miles away, and mom never said a word about this. I felt guilty that I was not there to make things better for her. I wish I would have called more often than just once a week. I wish I would have asked more questions. I wish, I wish …

When I think about mom, I see a strong, outgoing, and caring individual. Regardless of what was on her mind or what she had to deal with, mom almost always projected that she was a happy woman. She laughed, had a great sense of humor, could tell you joke after joke, enjoyed playing cards – I should say she mostly loved winning at cards – but her true love was music and dancing. When the right Bavarian polka or *Landler* would start playing on the radio, she swayed and, in her younger years if she was around other people, she would just grab someone and start dancing.

Mom had the most beautiful blonde and later white hair with natural waves, and she was very proud of it. I recall seeing her pull out a comb from under the pillow on the couch when someone came into the room to make sure she looked presentable. I remember how hard she worked all her life to overcome many obstacles; how she lived through the Depression and World War II; how she helped build her own home with her own two hands and stepped up to any challenge, including becoming the breadwinner when needed and nursing dad for the last years of his life. Mom stayed strong, even though I know her heart must have been breaking when my sister Freda, their grandchild Carola, and I all left Germany within a few months in 1963 to move to America, leaving her, my dad, and my 12-year-old brother behind.

When I think of mom, and that is often, I remember a caring mom, with a love for life. I close my eyes and see her drinking her coffee, smiling and swaying to the music. I see her hands weathered from hard work knitting socks, mittens, or something to make someone happy.

I wish I could see her one more time, hear her voice one more time, and hug her one more time. I am so grateful that she was my mom. I could not have asked for better, and I miss and love her with all my heart!

Mom and me

Chapter 28

Coming to America

In 1961, my sister Freda had met Pat, an American GI stationed in Baumholder, Germany. They were planning on getting married. Pat was coming to ask my parents for my sister's hand and brought his best friend, Steve, along for moral support.

There was an immediate attraction between Steve and me, and the next three days were like a whirlwind. On the third day he proposed.

I was barely 16 years old, had just graduated college, and was not crazy about Horst, the guy my parents wanted me to marry. I would have married Horst, because that's just the way it was in that little Bavarian village in the Alps. But now I had feelings I had never experienced before; and it was new, exciting, and beautiful. Oh dear, now how to convince my parents? Almost daily I would beg them to please support my choice. My parents were not bothered by the fact that I was Roman Catholic and Steve was Jewish; their concern was my age and moving to a foreign country. My dad somewhat struggled with the fact that he had been captured by the Americans during World War II.

The requests for permission to get married had now been going on for over a year. I was hoping that, at one point or another, my parents would remember the ordeal they went through to get my grandparents' blessing back in the day when they wanted to get married.

So, one day my dad asked all of us to leave so he could have a conversation with Steve to discuss matters. Between my dad's little bit of English and Steve's little bit of German, they came to some sort of understanding; and we finally got his blessing. I never found out what they discussed.

Steve, Dad and me

The next step was to get approval from the German court because I was underage. This was just the beginning; there was a ton of paperwork to be completed for the marriage and immigration.

Shortly thereafter I was asked to a meeting with Steve's Company Commander. Steve was his driver, so I thought it was just a formality or curiosity on his part. We chatted and periodically he would ask me a personal question. He ended the conversation by letting me know that he was happy for Steve and me and wished us well. I found out later that Steve's mother had contacted him and asked for his support in trying to stop the marriage.

Now reality set in that I was going to be living and raising a family in a foreign country. I had been concentrating on the romantic and consequently marriage side of this relationship and had ignored everything else. It hit me like a ton of bricks! First of all, I was entering into a possible hostile relationship with my future mother in-law, who was unhappy about her Jewish son marrying a Catholic German and had gone to great lengths trying to stop the marriage. But even more important, I needed to consider, if America should ever go to war with Germany, my children would have to fight against my brother's children. How would I deal with that? Could I deal with that? It was a horrifying thought! I agonized over this, had disturbing dreams, and finally tried to think about this as rationally as I could.

Bottom line, I was very much in love with this American soldier, and we wanted to get married. This meant leaving my family and my home in Germany to build a new life in America. I needed to be able to commit wholeheartedly to making the United States of America my home and becoming a responsible citizen.

I emigrated on May 3, 1963. My sister and I made a promise to each other that only English would be spoken in our homes for several reasons: we wanted to make sure her daughter Carola and any future children of ours would not be hindered in any way. We also wanted to perfect our English at the same time. Everything was foreign and new. Just translating spices for cooking was at times not an easy task. I still have to chuckle when I think of how long it took me to find out that *Muskatnuss*, a small nut I used to grate into bread dumplings as an added spice, came already ground and was called nutmeg.

Studying for the citizenship exam was the next hurdle. I studied hard, I was determined to learn as much as I could about the country of my choice and pass the citizenship exam on my first try. My husband, friends, and my sister-in-law Andrea helped me and quizzed me whenever there was an opportunity. Everything was good except naming the states; I always came up with one extra. We finally figured out that I included Arkansas twice, once the way it was written and then the way it was pronounced.

I passed my citizenship test with flying colors and was sworn in at the Dorothy Chandler Pavilion in Los Angeles on January 22, 1971.

I am so proud to be an American!

Chapter 29

Marita

I was born on Sunday, September 12, 1945, in Pfaffing by Chieming. I weighed 3.5 kilograms (7 lbs. 11 oz.). My mom wanted to call me Erna; she had tried that already with my sister and was overruled. And she was overruled again. I was baptized Maria Theresia, Maria after my godmother and Theresia after my grandmother. Mom just called me Marita which is comprised of the two names, and that's what everyone started calling me. I am glad mom lost on this one, I like my name and have often been told it is a pretty name. In 1971 as part of becoming a US citizen, I changed my name legally to Marita.

In this book you certainly read a lot about me. I wanted to just add a few little tidbits.

Willie Klier, a neighbor, did this pencil drawing of me when I was three years old. It has always been one of my favorites.

On November 12, 1952, I was rushed to the hospital with a burst appendix. When I woke up after the operation, I remembered that Egerer Opa was in the hospital as well, and I wanted to go see him. I got out of my bed and attempted to find him. When the nurse tracked me down, my stitches had ripped; I was scolded and put back in my bed. The stitches were not fixed, so to this day I have a very large scar as a reminder.

My school friends Anneliese, Monica, Rosl, Hildegard, Roswitha, Gisela, and I formed a Mickey Mouse Club. We were about seven or eight years old. All we did is sit in a tent at Anneliese's back yard, have fun, and tell stories and laugh while wearing Mickey Mouse hats. We developed such a deep friendship that each time I visited back home, my friends would organize a reunion. To this day we still stay in touch.

We had a wonderful gymnastic club in town owned by Frau Spazl. Anneliese, Rosl, Gisela, and I joined. Of course there was a fee, and the classes were all in the evening. Mom felt that was my consolation price for not being able to join the dance group. Frau Spazl was a very energetic and inspiring teacher. My favorite activities were working on the parallel bars. I was very limber back in those days.

In 1958 our entire class joined the Youth Olympics as did many clubs and even some schools. The competition incorporated three different sports including the parallel bars. I finished with 44 points and, even though it was not a national competition and I was not the winner or runner-up, I completed all the required activities and received my "*Sieger Urkunde*" (certificate of completion) signed by the President of the National Olympic Committee for Germany. This was something I was very proud of. It was my last summer in the gymnastics club because I started college in September.

The following picture was taken around the time Freda left for her job in Zweibruecken.

Freda was 14 years old; I was 10; and my brother was five. Because of the age difference, we never had close relationships with one another. My relationship with Freda developed and blossomed in America, for which I will be forever grateful.

Just before college graduation, I had to have my tonsils removed. Something happened with my vocal cords. I still remember how I was gently told that they could no longer use me in the choir at church.

My brother Manfred was about 12 when I left for America. I never had a lot of time with him growing up. Between work, school, and chores at home, there was not a lot of time and, because of the age difference, we had different interests. Of course there were times we had fun together, but there was never a lot of closeness. After Mal and I got married and went to Germany almost every two years from 1986 on, I was able to get to know Manfred better and treasure the times we had. During the last six months of his life, we exchanged many emails. Sadly, he passed on August 3, 2007, of asthma at the age of 56.

In writing this book, I have dealt with many different emotions. At times I would laugh out loud, remembering something funny. Or smile as I was thinking back on something special or people that touched my life. At other times, I felt very sad and missed my family tremendously. Tears fell when I thought back on what my mom experienced in the last six months of her life. I blamed myself for not having asked more questions, or the right questions, or for not calling more often than once a week. Sometimes I wished I could turn back the time and do things better. My heart aches for one more visit with my mom and dad, just one more smile or hug, or one more opportunity to hear their voices. Sometimes it was painful to remember the past, and I had to remind myself that all these memories are gifts!

Yes, the emotions ran high. I felt grateful for the friends and family that touched my life in so many ways. But mostly I felt so very lucky to have had my mom and dad as my parents to love me, teach me, prepare me for life, and support my choices. I could not have asked for better!

I am hoping you enjoyed reading about my childhood in beautiful Bavaria. I shared customs and traditions that mattered to me when I was growing up. Most important, I hope you got a glimpse of what I am all about, the traditions I treasure, the people I love, and why I love them so much.

I was truly blessed!

Chapter 30

The Promise

After Mal and I were married in 1986, we visited my parents almost every two years. Most of the time Freda would come with us, and we timed our visits to be there for either mom's or dad's birthday or one of their milestone anniversaries.

On a particular visit, I remember it was apparent that it was getting pretty tough for my parents to get around and do things. Dad had been in a wheelchair for many years by then; and mom was doing her best to take care of him, the house, and the daily responsibilities while dealing with debilitating arthritis and glaucoma herself. We always asked mom to prepare a chore list for us when we visited and tried to get as much done as we could – things like chopping and stacking wood, painting walls, major spring cleaning, and just fixing what needed to be fixed. Mom was always very grateful, but this one time mentioned that some of her friends were lucky to have their children close by.

Guilt feelings started to well up in me for not being there for my parents when it seemed they needed me most. I hugged mom and told her how very sorry I was. We cried and held each other. With tears still running down my face I went to dad and told him that I was sorry for having been so selfish by not taking their needs into consideration when I made the decision to move to America.

What happened next is what I call **a father's love**. Dad held my face in his hands and I can still hear him saying, *"Dirndl, weisst*

Du nicht, Du lebst doch meinen Traum!" which translates to "Girl, don't you know you are living my dream!" What a beautiful way to try to take away the guilt!

When saying our goodbyes, I always told my parents, "I will see you in two years." And the response always was, "We are looking forward to seeing you then." It was our way of making parting a little easier because we could count on the next visit.

In July 1998 we were there celebrating Dad's 88 birthday. His unexpected response to my normal "see you in two years" remark was that, if he would be looking forward to that, he would never have permission to die. I could not understand why he would respond that way, but at the same time the reality of mortality had set in. With a lump in my throat, I told him that I would be there for his 100th birthday whether he was there or not. Sadly, we lost him three months later, just nine months before their 60th wedding anniversary.

A promise is a promise, and I intended to keep what I promised. So Mal and I planned a visit to Chieming to be there on July 9, 2010, which would have been Dad's 100th birthday.

Mary and Larry Kunstler, longtime and very dear friends, were on a river cruise down the Rhine River. Upon completion of their cruise, they flew from Basel, Switzerland, to Salzburg, Austria, and joined Mal and me. We rented a car, and Larry became our very capable driver. We had a fabulous time exploring some of the places of my childhood.

Salzburg is the birthplace of Amadeus Mozart. I had been there many times before and was able to act as their guide. We sampled and enjoyed many of the Austrian specialties. We memorialized the trip with many photographs of all the fabulous sights.

One unforgettable trip we took was to Koenigsee, the deepest lake in Germany with the highest Alps that is known for the world-famous echo wall. If a trumpet is played or a horn is blown from a boat, the echo bounces back seven different times. Since 1909 only rowboats, pedal boats, or electric boats are allowed on this lake to keep pollution down.

We visited my brother's grave and spent a day at my sister-in-law Ingrid's restaurant in Siegsdorf. The regular traditional dancers were not performing that week, so Ingrid arranged for us to watch the youngest dancer group ages six to eight that were just learning dances at town square. It was so cute to see those children trying to learn the routine and some of the older kids stepping in at times to help them.

We stayed at Oberwirt in my hometown for several nights. I showed Larry and Mary the *Stammtisch*. This table is conspicuously marked as such with a big sign and is reserved for regulars. The men get together to play cards and are known often to have heated political discussions. After church on Sundays, you can also find them at the *Stammtisch* enjoying a *Fruehschoppen* (a morning beer). There are drawings on the walls of many of those men. One of our neighbors, Herr Klier, was an accomplished artist and did many of those drawings.

Each morning, we enjoyed a true Bavarian breakfast with fresh baked rolls, sweet butter, ham, eggs, jams and jellies, and fresh ground coffee. It was served in a room where dad had carved the pillars and the drapery rods. It was such a peaceful feeling to be somewhere that had a little of my dad in it.

I was honored that our friends Mary and Larry joined us in my hometown and wanted to know as much as possible about where I grew up. We explored Herreninsel and Fraueninsel and of course sampled Kloster liqueur made only at the cloister.

I enjoyed taking them to some of the special places of my childhood, however, it was bittersweet. Our house had been sold, and the new owner tore it down and built a new house. As we walked by the new house, I noticed a couple of mom's precious peonies sprouted up outside the new fence. I took it as a smile from mom. Many of the people I had known for so long had either moved away or joined my parents and brother in heaven. The town had changed. Bavarian owners of various restaurants or stores had been replaced by owners from other regions or countries, and my beloved Bavarian dialect was seldom to be heard.

On July 9, 2010, which would have been Dad's 100th birthday, I kept the promise I had made to Dad in 1988! We placed flowers on my parents' grave, including blue flowers, their favorite color. We ordered and attended the church service to honor dad. The service was attended by Mal, myself, my cousins Marita, Marianne, Lisbeth, Pauline, Agi and Erna, as well as Mary and Larry. Only two cousins, Christa and Antonia, were unable to come.

Front Row: Pauline, me, Marita, Agi, Erna, Mary & Larry
Back Row: Mal, Marianne & Lisbeth

After the service, we all had dinner at one of dad's favorite restaurants, The Strandwirt, by the lake. The food was as good as I remembered. Happily satisfied, we went on an after-dinner stroll along the lake and stopped for a cone of Dad's favorite green apple ice cream. It did not tickle my taste buds, but I looked up to heaven and said, "Dad, I hope you are enjoying this."

Now it was time for me to close the chapter and just treasure the memories. Mal took pictures of the beautiful sunset that appeared like it was specially ordered for the occasion. We watched as the sun slowly disappeared. It seemed like the perfect goodbye!